About the Author

❈

Martha Phelps Stamps is an eighth-generation Nashvillian who inherited a love for both cooking and writing from her mother. Martha began cooking professionally while she was an English student at the University of Virginia. At age twenty-eight, she followed her dream and entered the Culinary Institute of America, graduating with honors. After spending time on the island of St. John (at least it was warm), she made a prodigal return to Nashville, her family, and a serious cooking career.

While serving as chef at the Corner Market, Martha began writing about food for the *Nashville Scene.* She is the author of the cookbooks, *The New Southern Basics, Fall Harvests,* and *Spring Pleasures.* Martha and her husband, visual artist John Reed, began a successful catering business in 1999 and opened Martha's at the Plantation in 2000.

Martha has been featured in *Southern Living* and *Victoria* magazines, as well as on *Martha Stewart Living,* and the Food Network's *The Best Of.* Martha and John live in Nashville with their daughters, Moriah and Sadie; their son, John Mark; and Lady, the basset. They all eat well.

About the Artist

✳

John Reed, whose artwork adorns this book's cover, has painted for a lifetime and hopes to continue to do so. He studied at the Art Institute of Chicago and his work is collected around the country. Reed lives in Nashville with his wife Martha Phelps Stamps and three fantastic kids.

Martha's
at the
Plantation

Seasonal Recipes from
BELLE MEADE

Martha Phelps Stamps

Hill Street Press
Athens, Georgia

A HILL STREET PRESS BOOK

Published in the United States of America by
Hill Street Press LLC   191 East Broad Street, Suite 209   Athens, Georgia 30601-2848 USA
706-613-7200
info@hillstreetpress.com   www.hillstreetpress.com

Hill Street Press is committed to preserving the written word. Every effort is made to print books on acid-free paper with post-consumer recycled content. ❀ The recipes in this book require careful preparation and the use of proper ingredients. Neither the author nor publisher assumes any liability for the preparation and/or consumption of food prepared using the recipes in this book. ❀ No material in this book may be reproduced, scanned, stored, or transmitted in any form, including electronic and print media, or used without the prior written consent of the publisher. An excerpt not to exceed 5 recipes may be used one time only by newspaper/magazine editors in conjunction with a review/feature about the book, author, or Hill Street Press LLC. Attribution must be provided including the publisher, author name, and book title. ❀ Hill Street Press books are available in bulk purchase and customized editions to institutions/companies.

Text and cover design by Anne Richmond Boston.
Cover illustrations and cover photograph copyright © 2003 by John Reed.
Interior photographs courtesy of Beth Trabue.

Printed in the United States of America.

Library of Congress Cataloging-in-Publication Data

Stamps, Martha Phelps.
    Martha's at the plantation : seasonal recipes from Belle Meade / by Martha Phelps Stamps.
        p.   cm.
    Includes index.
    ISBN 1-58818-092-1 (hardcover : alk. paper)
    1. Cookery, American--Southern style. 2. Cookery--Tennessee. 3. Martha's at the Plantation
(Restaurant) 4. Belle Meade Plantation (Tenn.) I. Title.
TX715.5.S68S73 2003
641.5975—dc21   2003005275

ISBN#1-58818-092-1

10   9   8   7   6   5   4   3   2   1

First printing

For my husband, John Reed,
for being so foolishly romantic as to honestly believe
we could pull this whole thing off.

Contents

❋

Foreword

❈

The South is a place of ironic alliances and straightforward collaborations. Nowhere is this more evident than in the Southern kitchen.

The American antebellum plantation kitchen, where enslaved African women crossed their intelligence, aesthetics, and skills with the expectations, aesthetics, and ambitions of European plantation mistresses to create feasts of dizzying deliciousness, is a spicy example of the ironic alliance.

The feasts that Martha Stamps, a true Southern lady of the vanilla persuasion, concocts for me, a new Southern lady of the chocolate variety, honor (as they are informed by) all the women who have gone before—black and white, be they standing at the stove or sitting at the table—the women who created the Southern table. They are sweet examples of straightforward collaboration.

In the old Southern way, Martha turns simple meals into significant moments.

I celebrated the publication of my novel, *The Wind Done Gone,* with a Center-City (as opposed to country) supper of Martha's fried chicken and lima bean salad. A hundred happy, not-wanting-to-go-home guests later (from the outlaw singer/playwright Steve Earle to the original urban bad boy Jay MacInerney), I can attest that Martha's at the Plantation's food pleases the discerning urban palate.

At the other end of the spectrum, I entertained the Auction Committee of the Swan Ball (one of the last of the old-time, old-money, old-elegance institutions alive in America) with Martha's shrimp and grits, and was applauded by the committee for doing things "the way they used to be done, the way they should be done."

In Nashville everyone wants to celebrate their birthdays and their wedding showers at Martha's at the Plantation. On any given Saturday the bright glass room overlooking the grounds is *alive with* the chatter of bridesmaids, the squeals and giggles of grandchildren, and the low soft laughter of white heads that count friendship in decades and half-centuries. Now the rest of the country can join the feast.

When I start to think about Thanksgiving in late September, I take out my

❈

husband's family silver and start polishing. Then I make an appointment to go see Martha. We talk about the turkey, about frying and roasting and brining. We talk about the creamed onions, about the dressing, about the sweet potatoes—whether to use orange or bourbon, whether to puree or slice, whether to boil or bake. So many intersections and elaborations of experience and taste . . . so many questions.

The savoriest of the answers is in this book.

The South is a place where opposites are reconciled. A place where grace is not merely said, but tasted. When Martha Stamps cooks at the Plantation, she infuses her food with history and grace.

And that's a fine flavor for any home.

Alice Randall
Nashville, Tennessee 2003

Introduction

❈

There are facts, and then there are stories. I can tell you exactly how to cook something and make it work just right. Then I can tell you who told me, and why. For me, the who and why are usually the things that motivate my doing the what. Especially when it comes to food. Food carries pure emotion. Name a dish, and I can tell you where I was when I first tasted it, who I was with, and probably what I was wearing—akin to when man first landed on the moon or when John Lennon was shot. My first food memory is of fried peach pie (the back porch at my Grandmama's home, her housekeeper Catherine Couch, a blue gingham sundress). Every time I smell and taste a fried peach pie, or even think of one, I get a big, giant hug from Catherine Couch herself. And Couch could hug. If I go on a bit telling stories before my recipes, I guess that's why—I like a big hug, and assume that you might like to share one, too.

At times, our lives today seem so commonplace, our actions so by rote. Frozen pizza may sustain us to wake another day, but cooking something special lends us a connected-ness that I feel we all crave—to people and places and times perhaps remote from what we know now. Sharing food with others connects them as well. You can introduce your daughter to an uncle she never knew, and your mother to a friend you met in college. Or you can share a bit of how you felt—what you smelled and tasted, saw and heard in the woods one day when Mama spread out the old patchwork quilt, your sisters climbed trees, the trout lilies bloomed, and the creek ran clear and cold.

Although I rarely follow a recipe, owning a restaurant has required me to produce recipes for my staff to follow. So fear not—these recipes have been tested at Martha's, day in and day out. And while I don't consult them for recipes, I never, ever tire of reading cookbooks and finding inspiration from other people's food—especially if there's a story . . .

Here's a good one: I met my husband John in 1993 when I had just returned to my native Nashville. After two years of school in New York and eighteen

❈

months of heady misdirection living on the island of St. John in the West Indies, I had moved home full of purpose and ready to conquer the culinary scene. After a couple of months of miserable restaurant experiences, I found myself back at The Corner Market, Nashville's premiere "gourmet-grocery" and itinerant home to a multitude of creative types. John was just that—a thirty-something art student (former bass player) who was putting himself through school making sandwiches in the deli. I was immediately attracted to his scholarly dishevelment and his restored Triumph, yet we kept a respectful distance. We both had other commitments, and were on different paths. John earned a fellowship to the Art Institute of Chicago, and I became a mommy to Moriah and suddenly viewed life as one who had been blind.

Much later, when a mutual friend told me that John was back in town teaching school, and single, the old attraction stirred. I was newly independent as well, but in the throes of all which that implies.

Several months later I spied John from my perch behind the cheese counter, as he walked through the doors of The Corner Market seeking part-time work. I decided at once that our time had come, and relentlessly pursued the man until he agreed to marry me.

A month after we married I took on the position of executive chef at a small restaurant and helped the owners open a second restaurant the following spring. John was the coordinator of adult education at Cheekwood Fine Arts Center. We were soon expecting Sadie Anna. I was eight-months pregnant when it became apparent that, for a multitude of reasons, I could not resume my role at the restaurant after Sadie was born. I didn't know what I would do, but I had something called either blind faith or utter stupidity. The month was September and it occurred to me that many folks would be entertaining between then and Christmas. I sent out 200 cards to friends and former customers, announcing that I was ready to work. The response was so overwhelming that, by Thanksgiving, John had quit his job to work with me.

December was a huge success. Sadie had a crib at our catering kitchen. Our family helped out. We felt confident that we had made the right choices.

Then came January. Worse, then came February. But we had expected this— that catering would die on the vine after the holidays. We had a plan. Again we sent out direct mail—monthly newsletters featuring weekly menus available for home delivery—potpies and enchiladas, meat loaf and casseroles—homey stuff you could feed your kids. It worked. At least it paid the bills. All we had to do was write the menus, fold the menus, address the menus, stamp the menus, mail the menus, take the orders, buy the food, cook the food, package the food, label the food, invoice the food, deliver the food, wash the dishes, and mop the floors. We did it all. This was not necessarily the most stable period of our lives. We call it our growth stage.

In Nashville, catering starts up again in April, and we had quite our share of this business, as well as our home delivery one. In June we hired a close friend to help out now and then. Unfortunately, one pay period we had no money, so we paid her in leftover halibut. But it only happened once, and Katherine remains a very close friend. Things continued to improve, and Katherine received checks for her labor instead of fish. We were doing so well that in September we signed a lease on a tiny store front in the crappiest building in one of the best neighborhoods in town. We had it all figured out. Our lives were a precarious balancing act, but one that we had built. We were proud of ourselves.

A few days after we signed our new lease, I received a phone call from the director of Belle Meade Plantation. She was wondering if we would be interested in running the restaurant in the visitors' center. I was so embroiled in all we had planned that I almost said no. At least I had the sense to tell her that I would talk to my husband about it. John, as usual, set me straight. We planned a meeting to discuss the possibility.

Now for those of you who do not know, it can conservatively take upwards of $300,000 to open a restaurant. There are leases and equipment, staff and inventory, insurance and promotion. The possibility of our opening one was honestly nothing I had ever entertained, and here was Belle Meade Plantation, essentially offering us an almost new, beautiful facility in the very best neighborhood in town, complete with equipment. Not for free, of course, but in a package that made the intangible quite real. We could not have dreamed up a better match for ourselves than Belle Meade Plantation—my culinary penchant for the historical and local, our connections through both John's and my families' long standing involvement in the community, even John's experience in working with nonprofit museums and historical houses, and of course our catering background beautifully fit the needs of Belle Meade's tour groups and special events.

Still, there were plenty of hoops to jump through and precarious possibilities to overlook, but we had gotten good at that. I somehow failed to mention to John that we were expecting our third child, John Mark, until the ink had dried on our contract with Belle Meade. Baby John Mark spent his first year believing that all mommies smell like fried chicken, not a bad thought to take into your dreams. All said, and through it all, Big John Mark and I have had faith in one another and in some, at times, seemingly twisted order beyond our mere human comprehension.

Our greatest blessings have always lain in the ties of our humanity. Our families have supported us through tumult and celebration. Wonderful, amazing people both work with us and are our loyal customers. Last night, April 4, 2002, was the first night we opened our restaurant for dinner. Before I went home for the evening, I stepped into our beautiful dining room set with heavy linen, candlelight, and crystal to say good night to two of our most loyal customers and friends from the beginning. Paul stood up and gave me a great big hug. He looked straight into my eyes and said, "I can't tell you how exciting it's been for us to take this walk with you." John and I have felt his and Beth's, and so many others', presence every step of the way.

Our lives are all filled with a multitude of paths, and we all must eat along the way, so let's make it something good—maybe something your kids will tell their kids about. So turn the page, cook something special for someone you love, and start telling stories of your own.

Winter

Winter is the hunker-down time, when we all come together in a messy, noisy bunch. Winter's the essence of family time, really. First, of course, with the holidays, but then through those long cold months when there's not a whole lot to do. No fireflies to catch, no leaves to rake, no bulbs to plant, but lots of fires to watch and stories to tell. It's a marvelous time to cook, the kind of cooking that you don't want to do during other times of year. I like to braise and roast and simmer and stew. What wonderful smells, accented by burning wood and pine needles. The children love stew and potpie days, when the aroma welcomes them home. On Sundays I let them cook with me. Sadie very seriously pulls a chair to the counter, climbs up, and leans on my shoulder while Moriah peels and I chop. John Mark thoughtfully pulls each and every pot out of the cabinet and entertains us with his drumming. These are the days you're not sure if you're going crazy or having the time of your life. While I can I'll do the latter, and thank my lucky stars. I'll look at the seed catalogs when they've all gone to bed.

Cocktail Shrimp

I specifically call these tasty boiled shrimp because some shrimp, like the kind you buy precooked and frozen, define the opposite of tasty— tasteless. If you possibly have the time, do boil your own shrimp for cocktails and salads. Smaller shrimp I boil in the shell—the peel and eat variety. Really large shrimp, though, make such a beautiful presentation when they are peeled and deveined, and are imminently less messy. Just the thing for an elegant party. For sweet Sarah (my sister Mary's baby-sitter and friend) and Pat's wedding, we boiled 200 pounds! Now that was quite a celebration.

SERVES 6 TO 8.

4 ounces white wine vinegar
1 lemon, cut in half
1 small onion, cut in quarters
2 stalks celery, cut in half
4 sprigs celery
2 tablespoons salt

1 teaspoon cayenne pepper
2 pounds (16 to 20 shrimp), peeled and deveined shrimp (I like to leave the tail on, but it drives my father crazy—your choice)

In a large pot, bring 4 quarts of water to a boil. Add everything except the shrimp and simmer for 10 minutes. Add the shrimp and cook until they curl and become opaque, approximately 3 minutes. Remove the pot from the heat and add enough ice to stop the cooking. Let the shrimp rest in the cooking liquid for 5 minutes. Drain the shrimp and cool thoroughly before serving.

    I do not like to run water over the cooked shrimp because it washes away much of the flavor. However, it is important to get your shrimp cold in a hurry. If shrimp are still slightly warm after you drain them, place them in the refrigerator in a large uncovered bowl. Once they are cool, you may cover them with plastic and refrigerate until ready to serve. They may be cooked and refrigerated up to 4 hours before serving. Serve with cocktail sauce.

Crawfish Cakes with Rémoulade Sauce

We serve these as a lunch entree as well, but I like them best in a tiny bite-sized form for cocktail parties and the like. Crawfish is much less expensive than crab, and you will love the taste. At a party where 4 or 5 hors d'oeuvres are being served, the Crawfish Cake trays come back empty more quickly than anything else.

MAKES ABOUT 36 (1 1/2-INCH) CAKES

8 ounces butter

¼ red onion, diced

2 stalks celery, diced (including heart and leaves)

½ poblano pepper, diced

1 teaspoon chopped fresh garlic

¼ teaspoon Italian seasoning

1 pound frozen crawfish tails, thawed and drained

2 eggs, beaten

1 cup dry bread crumbs

Juice and zest of 1 lemon

1 tablespoon flat leaf parsley, roughly chopped

¾ teaspoon salt

¼ teaspoon black pepper

⅛ teaspoon cayenne

1½ tablespoons vinegar based cayenne hot sauce

Vegetable oil for frying

Rémoulade Sauce (recipe follows)

Melt the butter in a large sauté pan. Add the onion and cook for 3 minutes. Add the celery, poblano pepper, garlic, and Italian seasoning and cook 3 minutes more. Set aside.

Place the crawfish tails in the bowl of a food processor fitted with a steel blade. Pulse until the crawfish are very finely minced.

Place the sautéed vegetables and crawfish in a large mixing bowl, along with the remaining ingredients. Mix together thoroughly. Make a small "tester" cake and fry in a sauté pan in a small amount of oil. Taste and adjust seasoning. Form the mixture into small cakes, using a tablespoon. Place the cakes on a baking sheet. Cover and refrigerate at least 30 minutes.

Heat the oil in a deep fryer to 325°F. Fry the cakes for 3 minutes, until just cooked through. Drain and serve with Rémoulade Sauce.

Winter

Rémoulade Sauce

This is one of our most asked for (and useful) recipes. I simply hate to give it away! The secret is using really good mayonnaise and mustard.

MAKES 1 PINT.

1 cup Hellman's mayonnaise   1 cup Creole mustard

Mix together well. We store ours in a squirt bottle in the fridge for up to 1 week.

❄

Baked Brie with Pear and Cranberry Chutney

I have put this together for many cooking demonstrations. The presentation is beautiful and dramatic—also, very easy to do. This is a favorite for holiday celebrations.

SERVES 10 TO 12.

1 package (2 sheets) frozen puff pastry   1 egg yolk
1 whole 1½ pound brie   2 tablespoons milk
½ cup Pear and Cranberry Chutney (recipe
    follows)

Preheat oven to 400°F. Grease a baking sheet.
Let the puff pastry thaw for 30 minutes, according to package directions.
Use a knife to scrape the white layer off of one side of the brie.
Open 1 sheet of puff pastry and lay on a work surface. Spoon the chutney into the center of the pastry. Place the brie, scraped side down, on top of the chutney, and wrap the sides of the pastry up and around the brie. If necessary, cut pieces from the second sheet of pastry to patch the wrapped brie until it is fully encased.

❄

In a cup or small bowl, whisk the egg yolk together with the milk. Using a pastry brush, brush the egg mixture over the entire brie pastry.

Use a cookie cutter to cut decorative shapes from the remaining sheet of pastry. Apply the shapes to the egg-washed brie pastry, then brush the egg wash over the decorative shapes. Place on the prepared baking sheets and bake in the center of the preheated oven for 20 minutes, until puffed and brown. Let cool for 15 minutes before serving with sliced apples and pears.

appetizers

salads

soups

vegetables & sides

entrees

desserts & pastries

Pear and Cranberry Chutney

We use this chutney for so many things: we serve it on pork loin for dinner (divine with a Riesling!), stuff it into sweet potato biscuits along with salty country ham, and simply spoon it over a wedge of sharp white cheddar to serve along with crackers. We also sell it in jars for Christmas presents and other special occasions. This is a recipe you will honestly use a lot.

MAKES ABOUT 3 QUARTS.

5 firm, ripe pears, peel on, cut in ½-inch cubes
1 (1-pound) bag fresh cranberries, rinsed and left whole
1 red onion, diced
3 cups golden raisins
1½ pounds light brown sugar

2 cups cider vinegar
2 tablespoons mustard seeds
1 tablespoon whole cloves, tied in cheese cloth
2 teaspoons red pepper flakes
1½ tablespoons salt

Mix all of the ingredients together in a large non-reactive pot. Bring to a boil, stir, and turn heat to medium-low heat and simmer, stirring occasionally, for 1 hour. Let cool and store, covered, in the refrigerator, for up to 1 month.

Spinach Parmesan Balls

This is my version of a favorite hors d'oeuvre my mother frequently made when I was young. Several years ago I called her for the recipe, which she couldn't find. Together, we think we put it back together pretty well. We both agree that what really makes these work is using lots of black pepper.

You can make these ahead of time, freeze them, and heat them up when you have guests. They always make me think of happy winter holidays, when my sisters brought friends home from school. My mother has an unspoken rule that no one may be in her home for more than 1 minute without having a drink in one hand, and a nibble in another. The freezing ahead thing works for her (probably for you, as well).

MAKES ABOUT 36 BALLS.

1 (1-pound) box frozen spinach, thawed,
    drained, and squeezed very dry
4 tablespoons butter, melted
½ yellow onion, diced
2 teaspoons fresh garlic, chopped
½ teaspoon Italian seasoning

2 eggs, beaten
1 cup dry bread crumbs
1 cup shredded Parmesan cheese
1 teaspoon black pepper
1 teaspoon salt

Preheat oven to 375°F. Spray a baking sheet with nonstick spray.

Stir all the ingredients together in a large mixing bowl. Form the mixture into 1 1/2-inch balls and place 1 inch apart on the baking sheet. Bake for 15 minutes, until puffed and slightly brown. Serve warm.

Roasted Beef Tenderloin
Stuffed in Biscuits

Faboo and always so appropriate. Something you can count on, especially around the holidays, like a little black dress with your really good pearls.

We roast a lot of these for folks, and I am always happy to do it. I do feel obliged, however, to point out that there are really no tricks here: it's something you really can do yourself. I think that the meat is so expensive, many people are afraid they'll mess it up. Trust me, if you have a thermometer, you can roast anything!

STUFFS ABOUT 125 (2-INCH) BISCUITS IF THE TENDERLOIN IS SLICED THINLY. SERVES 8 TO 10 AS AN ENTREE.

1 beef tenderloin (approximately 5 pounds), chain and silver skin removed
Olive oil
Salt and pepper
Garlic powder

Preheat oven to 400°F. Line a roasting pan with a rack large enough to hold the tenderloin.

Rub the tenderloin with olive oil and generously season with the salt, pepper, and garlic powder.

Place the tenderloin on the rack-lined roasting pan and place all in the middle of the preheated oven. Roast for 30 minutes, until a meat thermometer registers 120°F in the middle of the thickest part of the loin. Let rest at least 10 minutes before slicing. (I like to refrigerate the tenderloin to cool it completely if I am slicing it thinly for stuffed biscuits or rolls.)

Serve the tenderloin warm or room temperature with horseradish sauce or grainy mustard.

Blue Cheese Straws

Cheese straws are without question one of my favorite nibbles throughout the year. They're especially handy at Christmas. The dough is a cinch to make in a food processor, then you can keep that handy in the fridge to slice and bake at will, or freeze the dough for goodness knows how long. Once they're baked the cheese straws will stay tasty for several days in an airtight tin—perfect to take to the office or to school as teachers' gifts.

MAKES ABOUT 50 SMALL WAFERS.

1 cup all-purpose flour
½ teaspoon baking powder
½ teaspoon salt
¼ teaspoon cayenne

4 ounces blue cheese, at room temperature
1 cup walnuts, pulsed to fine chop in a food processor
6 ounces butter, softened

Using a food processor, mix together the flour, baking powder, salt, and cayenne. Add the blue cheese, finely chopped nuts, and butter, and pulse to mix to a crumbly consistency. Gather the dough together with your hands and form into a rough log. Place in the center of a piece of film wrap, pull the wrap around the dough, and roll to make a log approximately 1 1/2 inches in diameter. Refrigerate at least 1 hour and up to 1 week.

Preheat oven to 350°F. Prepare a baking sheet with nonstick spray. Unwrap the dough and place on a cutting board. Slice off thin wafers and place 1/2-inch apart on the prepared baking sheet. Bake for approximately 10 minutes, until slightly browned. Let the wafers cool on the baking sheet before removing. Store in an airtight container for up to 1 week.

Black-Eyed Pea Salad

Winter

appetizers

salads

soups

vegetables & sides

entrees

desserts & pastries

This is one of the salads we served Martha Stewart when she was in town. Black-eyed peas are traditionally served for good luck on New Year's Day, so I think they make a perfect winter salad. Until recently, I had always used dried peas, which had to be soaked and cooked for a longer time. I find the frozen peas much more convenient. Of course, in the summer, fresh is the way to go.

SERVES 6 TO 8.

1 pound black-eyed peas (fresh or frozen)
1 bay leaf
2 teaspoons salt (plus additional to taste)
4 tablespoons olive oil
Juice and zest of 3 lemons
½ bunch scallions, sliced thinly

1 red pepper, roasted,
      skinned and seeded, and chopped
1 can chopped tomato, drained
1 chipotle pepper, finely copped
1 bunch flat leaf parsley, coarsely chopped
Freshly ground black pepper to taste

Rinse and pick over the peas. Place in a pot and cover with water. Add the bay leaf and salt and bring to a boil. Reduce heat to simmer and cook approximately 10 to 15 minutes for fresh, slightly longer for frozen. (They should be completely cooked through, but not at all mushy.)

Drain the cooked peas in a colander, then place the peas in a mixing bowl, pour the olive oil and lemon juice over them while still warm. Let cool to room temperature without stirring. Remove the bay leaf and stir in the remaining ingredients. Adjust seasoning and serve.

May be made a day in advance. Let the salad come to room temperature before serving.

Winter

Warm Beet and Potato Salad with Crumbled Blue Cheese

I served this salad at a bridal luncheon for Katherine, our pastry chef and fellow beet person, and it was a huge hit. I know that people are often reluctant to serve dishes that are prone to evoke strong opinion, but I think that it is usually a welcome change of pace. Just offer something a bit more accessible as well and everybody's happy!

SERVES 8.

1 cup frozen pearl onions

1 tablespoon plus 3 tablespoons olive oil

4 medium beets

4 Yukon gold potatoes, peeled and cut into sixths

2 tablespoons rice wine vinegar

Salt and pepper

4 cups field greens

4 ounces crumbled blue cheese

Place the pearl onions on a baking sheet. Pour 1 tablespoon of olive oil over the onions and toss with a little salt and pepper. Roast in the center of the preheated oven for 10 minutes. Remove from the oven and set aside.

Rinse and trim the beets. Place in a sauce pan and cover with water. Bring to a boil and cook over medium-high heat until the beets are tender. Drain the beets. When they are cool enough to handle, peel the beets and cut into sixths in wedges. Place in a mixing bowl and set aside.

Place the potatoes in a sauce pan and cover with salted water. Bring to a boil and cook over medium-high heat until tender, about 10 minutes. Drain the potatoes and add to the mixing bowl, along with the pearl onions, remaining olive oil and rice wine vinegar. Mix gently and season to taste with salt and pepper.

Divide the greens among 8 salad plates and top with the warm salad. Finish with blue cheese and serve at once.

Chicken Noodle Salad

This is one of my husband's favorite salads. The flavors are so bright and fresh. It makes a welcome light supper on the coldest of nights. For our vegetarian friend Bob's fortieth birthday, I made it with fried tofu instead of chicken, and it was delicious as well.

SERVES 8.

1 tablespoon plus 2 tablespoons vegetable oil
2¼ pounds boneless, skinless chicken breasts
Salt and pepper
1 (8-ounce) package rice noodles
¼ head red cabbage, shredded
2 cups broccoli florets, sliced thin
1 carrot, shredded
½ red onion, sliced thinly

2 tablespoons soy sauce
2 tablespoons rice wine vinegar
Juice of 1 lime
1 teaspoon sesame oil
1 tablespoon toasted sesame seeds
2 tablespoons sunflower seeds
2 tablespoons chopped fresh mint

Preheat the oven to 400°F.

Heat 1 tablespoon vegetable oil in an ovenproof, nonstick sauté pan. Season the chicken breasts with salt and pepper and place in the heated oil. Cook for 2 minutes, turn and cook for 2 more. Place the pan in the oven and cook 5 minutes more. Remove from the oven and set aside. When cool enough to handle, shred the chicken into bite-sized pieces. Place in a large mixing bowl and set aside.

Cook the noodles according to package directions. Drain and cool under running water. Drain very well, then place in the mixing bowl along with the remaining ingredients. Toss well, and season to taste. Let the salad sit for 30 minutes to allow the flavors to marry. Toss again and serve.

Barley Salad with Apples and Wilted Red Cabbage

This is a slightly unusual salad that's loaded with flavor and texture, as well. It makes a wonderful and very pretty winter luncheon.

SERVES 6 TO 8.

1½ cups pearl barley
3 tablespoons olive oil
½ red onion, sliced thinly
4 cups red cabbage, shredded
1 Granny Smith apple, cored and
    sliced into thin wedges

2 tablespoons red wine vinegar
1 tablespoon brown sugar
2 scallions, sliced thinly

Cook the barley in a large pot of boiling salted water until tender, about 40 minutes. Drain thoroughly and rinse under cold water. Toss with a little olive oil to keep it from sticking and set aside.

Heat the olive oil in a sauté pan. Add the onion and cook on medium high for 4 minutes. Add the cabbage and cook to wilt, about 3 minutes, stirring occasionally. Add the apples and cook 2 minutes more. Stir in the vinegar and brown sugar. Add the cooked barley and toss thoroughly. Serve warm, topped with the sliced scallions.

Fried Sweet Potato Salad

Winter

What do you do when Fried Green Tomato Salad season is over? Declare it official Fried Sweet Potato Salad season. Of course, we Southerners will fry anything. And if you put it on a bed of greens, it must be healthy.

The trick to this is slicing the sweet potatoes very thin or in tiny matchsticks. Sweet potatoes have such a high moisture content that they don't fry easily, so the more surface that actually touches the oil, the better.

SERVES 6.

1 cup frozen black-eyed peas
1 tablespoon olive oil
Salt and pepper
2 sweet potatoes, cut into match sticks, or
    very thinly on a mandolin
Vegetable oil for frying

8 cups field greens
8 ounces Lemon-Thyme Vinaigrette
    (see page 85)
½ cup Creamy Horseradish Sauce
    (see page 168)

Preheat oven to 400°F.

Pour the black-eyed peas onto an unprepared baking pan. Toss the peas with the olive oil and a pinch of salt and pepper. Roast in the center of the preheated oven for 10 minutes. Remove and set aside.

Heat the oil in a deep fryer to 335°F. Fry the sweet potatoes until golden brown and crispy, making sure that they are all browning and not sticking together. (You may have to fry in batches, depending on the size of your fryer.) Drain well on paper towels or clean brown paper bags.

In a large bowl, toss the greens with the Lemon-Thyme Vinaigrette. Divide evenly among 6 plates. Top with the fried sweet potatoes and roasted black-eyed peas. Drizzle with Creamy Horseradish Sauce and serve at once.

Red Beans and Rice

I first encountered red beans when I worked with my friend Steve Scalise, who taught me so much about Cajun and Creole food. He taught me the most important essence of a good bowl of red beans— they should be creamy and smooth, not chewy or broken up. Now, I do a couple of things Steve never did with his beans that I have picked up along the way. And while Steve will tell you these steps are utter nonsense and completely unnecessary (I have edited Steve's language a bit), I find that they give me a more consistent product every time.

First of all, I always soak my beans. Not only does this give you a head start on your cooking, but soaking and then rinsing the beans will eliminate a lot of the impurities that cause gas, embarrassing to some, quite painful to others.

My other little tip is not to add salt until the beans are almost done. My Italian chef in culinary school, Claudio Papini, told me that this would keep the beans from breaking and becoming tough. I've tried it both ways, and I'm with chef Papini, a brilliant man who taught me the difference between being a chef and being a cook.

Anyway, red bean cooking is a simple, albeit long, process. In New Orleans beans were traditionally cooked on wash day. You did a load of laundry, you stirred your beans. You did a load of laundry, you stirred your beans. So don't forget to stir your beans! They'll scorch on you and break your heart. But when your beans turn creamy smooth, they're just so good they'll make you cry.

SERVES ABOUT 16.

4 cups red kidney beans, picked over,
    rinsed, and soaked in water overnight
1 yellow onion, chopped medium
2 poblano peppers, chopped
3 ribs celery, chopped
1 (28-ounce) can chopped tomatoes, with
    juice
2 teaspoons Italian seasoning
1 pound Andouille or kielbasa sausage, cut
    into ½-inch circles

1 tablespoon salt
1 teaspoon black pepper
Vinegar-based hot sauce, to taste
¼ cup fresh parsley, chopped
1 tablespoon butter
1 cup long grain rice
2 cups water
¼ cup thinly sliced green onions

Drain the beans and rinse again. Place in a large pot and cover by double their volume with water. Bring to a boil, stir and skim off any scum that rises. Turn heat to low and cook, stirring occasionally, for 1 hour. Add the onion, poblano pepper, and celery. Stir and continue to cook, stirring occasionally, for 1 more hour, adding water as necessary to keep the beans from scorching. Stir in the tomatoes with their juice and the Italian seasoning. Continue to cook the beans, stirring occasionally.

appetizers

salads

soups

vegetables & sides

entrees

desserts & pastries

Preheat the oven to 400°F. Spread the sausage out on an unprepared baking pan and roast in the center of the oven for 10 minutes. Remove from the oven and drain the sausage well. Stir the drained sausage into the beans. When the beans are soft, and the broth is becoming creamy, you may stir in the salt and pepper, and hot sauce. When the beans are completely soft and the broth is nice and creamy, they are done! Stir in the parsley and keep the beans warm while you cook the rice.

Melt the butter in a medium sauce pan. Add the rice and stir to coat. Pour in the water and stir once. Bring the water to a boil, stir again, turn the heat to very low, cover, and cook for 15 minutes. Remove the lid and spread the rice out on a sheet pan to cool slightly before fluffing with a fork.

To serve, spoon a little rice into individual bowls and ladle the beans over the rice. Garnish with green onions and serve with extra hot sauce.

Winter

Potato and Cabbage Soup
with Country Ham

This soup is like good country music. Humble, no frills, and good for what ails you.

SERVES 10 TO 12.

3 tablespoons olive oil
1 yellow onion, chopped
2 carrots, diced
2 stalks celery, diced
2 teaspoons chopped fresh garlic
3 sprigs fresh thyme
   (or ½ teaspoon dried)
½ head green cabbage, shredded
   and chopped
8 cups chicken stock, heated

½ pound country ham steak,
   cut into 3 or 4 pieces
3 Yukon gold potatoes, peeled
   and sliced thinly
2 tablespoons vinegar-based
   hot sauce
Salt and pepper to taste
Red onion, diced, to garnish
Fresh parsley, diced, to garnish

Heat the olive oil in a large soup pot. Stir in the onion and cook for 4 minutes. Add the carrots, celery, garlic, and thyme and cook 5 minutes more. Add the cabbage, cook 1 minute, then pour in the stock, and add the country ham. Bring to a boil, add the potatoes, and cook over medium heat until the potatoes are falling apart, approximately 10 to 15 minutes.

Fish out the country ham, discard the gristle or bone, shred the meat and add back to the pot. Add the hot sauce and salt and pepper to taste. Garnish with diced red onion and parsley.

Turkey Succotash

Winter

I made this for my friend Alice when she wanted an easy cold weather supper with a little Southern attitude. I liked it so much, I made extra and served it for my mama's birthday.

Turkey is such a superior fowl to chicken, and so underused. Especially if you're using the turkey to make stew or gumbo, you don't have to fuss with the roasting to get the perfect looking bird. I roast a turkey on its breast, so all of the yummy fat from the back and thighs seeps down to tenderize and moisten the white meat. Just season the thing, and it will practically cook itself.

Once, when I was really busy, I put a turkey in the oven when I was going to bed, and set my alarm clock for when it needed to come out. As a culinary role model, I shouldn't urge you to cook while you are sleeping, but you get the idea. Cooking a turkey is not rocket science, and it tastes so fine. Of course, you could buy cooked turkey from the store, but it will never be exactly the same.

SERVES 6 TO 8.

3 tablespoons olive oil
1 yellow onion, diced
2 poblano peppers, cored, seeded, and diced
2 carrots, peeled and diced
2 ribs celery, diced
2 teaspoons chopped fresh garlic
½ teaspoon Italian seasoning
4 cups chicken stock, heated
1 cup frozen lima beans

1 cup frozen black-eyed peas
1 cup frozen corn
1 (14½-ounce) can roasted red peppers, drained and chopped
½ pound cooked turkey, shredded
1 tablespoon red wine vinegar
2 tablespoons chopped flat leaf parsley
Salt and pepper to taste
2 green onions, sliced thinly

Heat the olive oil in a large pot. Add the onion and cook on medium high for 4 minutes. Add the poblano peppers, carrots, celery, garlic, and Italian seasoning, and cook 5 minutes more. Pour in the chicken stock and bring to a boil. Add the lima beans and black-eyed peas, and cook on medium for 10 minutes. Add the corn and roasted peppers, bring back to a boil, and simmer for 5 minutes. Stir in the turkey and heat through. Add the red wine vinegar, then taste and adjust the seasoning with salt and pepper. Stir in the parsley and green onion and serve.

Chicken, Shrimp, and Sausage Gumbo

I have always shied away from writing down a recipe for gumbo. There are so many different kinds, and I have borrowed tidbits from every gumbo I've ever tried. This is the gumbo I most frequently make, because these are the meats I am most likely to have lying around.

You may notice that I use oil in my roux instead of butter. I learned this from my friend Pat Boudreaux, an honest to goodness Cajun lady, who told me it was all she ever used—and she used simple corn oil. I upgraded to olive oil because I like the taste. I like it better than butter because olive oil can get hotter and make your roux browner with less likelihood of burning.

People who tell me they like my recipes because they use so few ingredients will be disappointed here—but I simply cannot help it. A lot of good stuff goes into making gumbo. It's just as complex as the people who make it.

SERVES 12 TO 15.

1 yellow onion, diced

3 stalks celery, diced

2 green peppers, cored, seeded, and diced

1 tablespoon fresh chopped garlic

1 teaspoon dried thyme leaves

1 teaspoon dried rosemary, crushed

3 bay leaves, crushed

¼ teaspoon cayenne

2 tablespoons filé powder

1 tablespoon salt

½ teaspoon black pepper

1 cup olive oil

1 cup flour

4 quarts shrimp or lobster stock (or chicken, if you have to), heated

1 pound Andouille sausage, sliced into 1-inch rounds

1 (28-ounce) can chopped tomatoes, with juice

4 cups cooked chicken, shredded

3 pounds (16 to 20 count) shrimp, peeled and deveined

2 tablespoons vinegar-based hot sauce

1 bunch green onions, sliced thinly

4 tablespoons flat leaf parsley, roughly chopped

Winter

Place the chopped vegetables, spices, salt, and pepper in a large soup pot. Stir together well, cover, and place over very low heat.

Place the olive oil in a large sauté pan. Whisk in the flour and cook over medium heat, whisking now and then, until the roux is the color of coffee ice cream. At this point you should whisk constantly, continuing to cook, until the roux is the color of a new-ish copper penny.

Remove the lid from the vegetables and carefully (nothing burns like roux—it's kind of like lava—so watch out!) pour the roux over the vegetables in the pot. This will splatter and sizzle in a grand fashion. Stir it all together very well, then place the pot over medium-high heat.

Now pour half of the heated stock into the roux, stirring constantly. When this is all incorporated, stir in the remaining stock.

While the gumbo is cooking, preheat the oven to 400°F. Place the Andouille in a baking pan and roast for 15 minutes, until the sausage is slightly brown and has given off much of its fat. Remove from the oven and drain the sausage well.

When the gumbo has come to a boil, add the tomatoes with their juice, and bring back up to a boil.

Now add the chicken, shrimp, and sausage, and turn off the heat. Let the gumbo sit for 10 minutes, then stir in the hot sauce, green onions, and parsley. Taste to adjust seasoning and serve over cooked long grain rice.

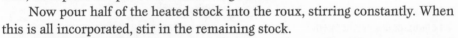

Butternut Squash Soup
with Maple and Granny Smith Apples

This soup is a cinch to make, with a rather refined result. I prefer it to most creamy soups because there's no cream in it at all, so it's lighter than you would expect. The flavor is really nicely balanced with the tart apples and sweet maple syrup.

The hardest part of this soup is prepping the squash—make sure your knife is really sharp.

SERVES 10 TO 12.

1 butternut squash, peeled and cut into cubes	Salt
1 red onion, coarsely chopped	White Pepper
3 Granny Smith apples, peeled, cored and roughly chopped	3 tablespoons maple syrup
	3 quarts chicken stock, heated
4 tablespoons butter, cut in pieces	Juice of 2 lemons

Preheat the oven to 375°F. Place an oversized piece of aluminum foil in a 9 x 11-inch or comparable baking dish. Put the squash, onion, apple, and butter pieces in the center of the aluminum foil. Season generously with salt and white pepper, and enclose inside the foil. Place in the center of the preheated oven and roast for 1 hour, until the squash is quite tender. Carefully open the foil. (Don't get burned by the escaping steam!) Drizzle the maple syrup over the roasted vegetables, reseal the foil, and return to the oven for 20 minutes more. Remove the pan with the vegetables from the oven, loosen the foil, and set aside.

When the roasted vegetables are cool enough to handle, place small amounts in a blender along with equal parts warm chicken stock. Puree and pour into a sauce pan. When all of the squash is pureed, cook over medium heat until completely heated through. Add the lemon juice and taste for seasoning.

Beet Root Soup with Fennel

If you know me, you know I like beets. Actually, I love them. I will take any excuse to put them on any menu, and have been accused of being a bit preachy in my vigilant quest for converts. Methodists are usually uncomfortable with being called preachy, but I'll go out on a limb for beets.

This soup is such the winter tonic. Delicious and heart warming, and so darn good for you, it's crazy. That's why I garnish it with sour cream. It's just crazy without it.

SERVES 6 TO 8.

2 tablespoons olive oil
½ red onion, sliced thinly
2 stalks celery with leaves, sliced thinly
2 carrots, peeled and thinly sliced
3 medium beets, peeled and thinly sliced
2 quarts chicken stock
1 teaspoon salt

½ teaspoon crushed red pepper
Pinch crushed fennel seeds (about 6 to 10 seeds)
1 tablespoon rice wine vinegar
1 tablespoon honey
¼ cup sour cream
2 green onions, thinly sliced

Heat the olive oil in a soup or stock pot. Add the onion and cook over medium-high heat for 4 minutes. Add the celery, carrots, and beets and cook another 5 minutes. Add the stock and bring to a boil. Turn heat to low and cook until the beets are tender and starting to fall apart. Season with the salt, pepper, and fennel seeds and simmer 5 minutes. Stir in the rice wine vinegar and honey and remove from the heat. Taste and adjust seasoning.

Ladle the soup into individual bowls and garnish with a teaspoon of sour cream and a bit of sliced green onion.

Winter

appetizers

salads

soups

vegetables & sides

entrees

desserts & pastries

Winter Squash Puree

This is a beautiful dish, brilliantly golden in color. I like to put it on a buffet for this very reason. That, and it's delicious. I think that some people are intimidated by winter squash's tough exterior, but this is really simple to prepare. You just have to cut the squash in half. After roasting, the flesh pulls away from the shell quite easily. If you haven't done much with hard squash, this is a good recipe to try.

SERVES 4 TO 6.

2 pounds butternut or acorn squash
2 tablespoons plus 2 tablespoons olive oil
Salt and pepper
1 teaspoon fresh chopped garlic

2 teaspoons fresh chopped ginger
Juice of 1 lemon
½ cup milk, heated

Preheat oven to 400°F. Slice the squash in half and scoop out the seeds. Drizzle the flesh with 2 tablespoons of the olive oil and season with salt and pepper. Place flesh side down in a baking dish. Pour in 1/2 cup water to keep the squash from scorching. Bake for approximately 45 minutes to 1 hour, until the squash is quite soft. Remove from the oven and let the squash slightly cool.

Heat the remaining olive oil in a sauté pan and add the garlic and ginger, cooking on low heat for 5 minutes. Set aside.

When the squash is cool enough to handle, use a spoon to scrape the flesh from the shell. Run the squash through a food mill, or press it through a sieve. Place in a mixing bowl, along with the olive oil, garlic, ginger, lemon juice, and heated milk. Mix together well, and taste for seasoning.

Serve warm.

Braised Red Cabbage

Winter

This cabbage is really wonderful with winter's slow-cooked meats, like brisket or pork roast. The sweet and sour taste balances perfectly with rich-tasting meats and game—I love it with dark turkey meat.

SERVES 6 TO 8.

3 tablespoons olive oil
½ red onion, sliced very thinly
1 head red cabbage, outer leaves
    and core removed, sliced
    very thinly

¼ cup water
2 tablespoons cider vinegar
1 tablespoon brown sugar
2 tablespoons black currants
Salt and pepper to taste

Heat the olive oil in large sauté pan. Add the onion and cook on medium-high heat for 4 minutes. Add the cabbage and toss well, coating the cabbage with olive oil. Bring the heat back up in the pan, then add the water, cider vinegar, and brown sugar. Turn the heat to low, cover and cook for 20 minutes. Add the currants and cook another 5 minutes. Season to taste with salt and pepper. Serve warm.

Barley and Spinach Risotto

When I got to the Plantation, I really wanted to do some things with barley, because we know that barley was one of Belle Meade's main crops. But I sometimes find barley a bit slimy. This "risotto" takes advantage of barley's gooey traits. It's not really a risotto, which is a rice dish from northern Italy, but the barley is creamy and rich, just like a good risotto. Perfect for a chilly night.

SERVES 6 TO 8.

4 tablespoons olive oil	½ teaspoon salt
½ yellow onion, chopped fine	½ teaspoon black pepper
1 cup pearl barley	6 to 7 cups chicken stock, heated
½ cup white wine	8 ounces baby spinach
1 tablespoon fresh chopped garlic	½ cup Parmesan cheese

Heat the olive oil in a sauce pan. Add the onion and cook over medium-high heat for 2 minutes. Add the barley and stir to coat. Add the wine, garlic, salt, and pepper. Cook, stirring, until the wine is evaporated.

Begin to add the chicken stock, about 1 cup at a time. Stir and let the barley simmer until the stock is almost completely evaporated.

Continue adding the stock in 1 cup increments until the barley is tender, approximately 45 minutes to 1 hour. Stir in the spinach and Parmesan, taste for seasoning and serve warm.

Cauliflower Gratin

Martha's first chef, John Stephenson, came up with a similar dish for our first winter menu. Pungent cauliflower and smokey bacon are made for each other, and what's not better with sharp cheddar cheese?

SERVES 4 TO 6.

1 pound cauliflower florets
2 slices bacon
2 tablespoons butter
½ yellow onion, chopped fine
1½ cups cream

1 teaspoon salt
½ teaspoon white pepper
Pinch nutmeg
¼ cup bread crumbs
½ cup white cheddar cheese

Preheat oven to 375°F. Spray a 2-quart baking dish with nonstick spray.

Bring a pot of salted water to a boil. Add the cauliflower and cook until just tender, approximately 5 minutes. Drain, place in a mixing bowl, and set aside.

Cook the bacon in a sauté pan until it has rendered most of its fat. Remove the bacon and discard. Add the butter and heat. Add the onion and cook on medium-high heat until soft, approximately 5 minutes.

Add the onions to the cauliflower and mix well. Pour into the prepared baking dish.

Stir the cream with the salt, pepper, and nutmeg. Pour over the cauliflower, top with the bread crumbs, and then the cheese. Bake uncovered until the cream is absorbed or evaporated, and the top is crispy brown, approximately 40 minutes. Serve warm.

Pan-Seared Grits

We use this as the base for many stews and braised dishes. It's not puffy like our Baked Cheese Grits, but crunchy on the outside and creamy within. It's one of my favorite side dishes, any time of year.

SERVES 4 TO 6.

4 cups milk	1 cup yellow grits or polenta
1 teaspoon salt	½ cup grated Parmesan cheese
½ teaspoon black pepper	1 tablespoon olive oil

Prepare an 8 x 12-inch, or comparable, baking pan with at least 1-inch sides, by spraying with nonstick spray. Heat the milk with the salt and pepper. Bring to a simmer and whisk in the grits. Cook on medium heat, stirring, until the mixture thickens, approximately 5 minutes. Stir in the Parmesan cheese. Pour the mixture onto the prepared baking pan and spread evenly. Cover with plastic wrap and refrigerate at least 1 hour, or overnight.

Remove the plastic wrap and cut the chilled grits into triangles or squares, depending on your taste.

Heat the olive oil in a nonstick sauté pan. Add the grits pieces (You may have to do this in 2 batches), and cook on medium-high heat without turning for 4 minutes. Turn and cook a couple of minutes more. Serve warm.

Brussels Sprouts with Bread Crumbs and Garlic

I am wont to proselytize on the merits of Brussels sprouts as much as I do on those of beets. The first winter we opened, we used sprouts as our "veg of the day." For every person who turned up their nose, there were 10 who praised us for the courage to serve something "controversial." I got talked out of serving Brussels sprouts last year, in an attempt to appeal to the masses. But they're back now, baby. I can't appeal to everyone, any more than a Brussels sprout can. But I still think more people would love them if they'd just give them a chance.

SERVES 6 TO 8.

2 pounds Brussels sprouts, trimmed and
    cut in half
2 tablespoon olive oil
½ teaspoon salt
½ teaspoon black pepper

2 teaspoons fresh chopped garlic
2 tablespoons white wine
2 tablespoons plus 1 tablespoon bread
    crumbs

Bring a pot of salted water to a boil. Add the Brussels sprouts and cook until just tender, approximately 5 minutes. Drain and cool under cold running water. Brussels sprouts may be prepared to this point up to a day in advance.

Preheat the broiler 20 minutes before serving.

Heat the olive oil in an ovenproof sauté pan. Add the Brussels sprouts, salt, pepper, and garlic and toss well. Add the white wine and cook until the wine is evaporated and the Brussels sprouts are quite tender, approximately 5 minutes. Add the 2 tablespoons bread crumbs and toss to coat. Top with the remaining bread crumbs and run under the broiler until toasty brown, approximately 1 minute. Serve warm.

Beef Potpie

Every year, a few of my closest friends get together for a small and casual celebration of accomplishments past and prospects yet to come. It's my favorite party of the season—one evening I know that I can actually relax and enjoy myself. One of the reasons is that we always serve something savory, simple, and utterly satisfying, such as this Beef Potpie. It may be made ahead of time up until the time of baking, when you just pop it into the oven.

SERVES 4 TO 6.

2 pounds stew beef

2 tablespoons plus 2 tablespoons olive oil

Salt and pepper

2 tablespoons flour

3 tablespoons plus ½ cup red wine

2 tablespoons butter

1 yellow onion, chopped

4 cloves garlic, minced

2 cups beef or chicken broth, heated

2 medium turnips, peeled and chopped

3 carrots, peeled and chopped

4 small new potatoes, quartered

1 teaspoon chopped fresh rosemary, or ½ teaspoon dried

1 tablespoon corn starch (optional)

1 recipe piecrust (see page ???)

1 egg yolk

1 tablespoon milk

Trim the stew beef. I usually also cut the pieces smaller than they come from the store, so that they'll cook more quickly. Heat the oil in a deep skillet or Dutch oven on top of the stove. Sprinkle the trimmed beef with salt and pepper, then flour. Brown the beef on all sides, being careful not to overcrowd the pan. You may need to do this in batches.

Remove the browned pieces from the skillet and deglaze with 3 tablespoons of the red wine, stirring up any bits of browned meat. Let the wine reduce for 30 seconds, then pour out and reserve. Wipe out the skillet or Dutch oven well. Place the pan back on the stove and melt the butter. Cook the onion in the butter on medium-high heat until translucent, about 4 minutes. Add the garlic and cook 1 more minute. Add the beef back to the skillet along with the broth and remaining wine. Bring to a simmer. Turn the heat to low and cook about 1 to 1

1/2 hours, until the beef is just tender. Add the remaining vegetables, along with the rosemary, and additional salt and pepper to taste. Cook until quite tender and the liquid is well reduced, about 1 hour more. If the liquid is runnier than you like, mix the corn starch in a small cup with 1 tablespoon water. Stir into the simmering stew. When the stew comes back to a simmer, it will thicken the broth.

Pour the stew into a deep pie pan. Top with the pastry and vent it with some slits or decorative cutouts. Make an egg wash with the yolk and milk and use a pastry brush to paint over the pie. Bake until the crust is nicely browned, about 15 to 20 minutes. Serve warm with a big green salad and a simple, robust red wine, such as Rioja or Côtes du Rhone.

Winter

appetizers

salads

soups

vegetables & sides

entrees

desserts & pastries

Stacked Tortillas with Shredded Pork and Salsa Verde

Our friend and loyal customer Ann Buchanan has promised me that she will buy 50 books if I include this recipe. So Ann, this one's for you!

This was actually a favorite with lots of our customers back in our home-delivery days. The pork is slow cooked before it's shredded. If you haven't much time, BBQ pork from the store or the BBQ stand can be used, as well.

SERVES 8 TO 10.

1 boneless Boston pork butt
   (about 4 pounds)
1 tablespoon salt
1 tablespoon black pepper
1 tablespoon plus 1 tablespoon ground
   cumin
1 tablespoon plus 1 tablespoon chili powder
1 tablespoon oregano
2 tablespoons plus 2 tablespoons olive oil
2 teaspoons garlic powder
1 yellow onion, chopped
2 poblano peppers, cored, seeded and
   chopped

1 tablespoon fresh chopped garlic
1 (28-ounce) can chopped tomatoes with
   juice
1 chipolte pepper, minced, with 2
   tablespoons adobo sauce
1 cup sour cream
Corn tortillas
2 cups Salsa Verde (recipe follows)
1½ cups crumbled Queso Frico
   (Spanish dry white cheese) or feta

Preheat the oven to 325°F. Rub the pork roast with salt, pepper, 1 tablespoon cumin, 1 tablespoon chili powder, and the oregano. Heat 2 tablespoons olive oil in a large ovenproof pot. Add the pork and brown on all sides. Cover the pot and place it in the oven. Cook until the meat is quite tender and easy to shred, about 3 to 3 1/2 hours. Let the pork rest until cool enough to handle, then shred into pieces. Wrap and reserve half of the pork for another use. You can refrigerate it for up to 3 days or freeze it, well wrapped, for up to a month. Refrigerate the portion you will be using until it is called for in the recipe. Discard the fat from the pan juices, strain the juices, and set aside.

Heat the remaining olive oil in a deep sauté pan or Dutch oven. Add the onion and cook on medium high for 4 minutes. Add the poblano pepper, garlic, and the remaining cumin and chili powder, and cook 5 minutes more. Add the tomatoes and chipolte and continue to cook for 5 minutes. Stir in the shredded pork and the sour cream and heat through (do not boil, or the sour cream might separate). Remove from the heat.

Preheat the oven to 350°F. Spray a 4-quart casserole dish with nonstick spray.

Place tortillas overlapping in the bottom of the casserole. Layer in half of the pork mixture. Make another layer of tortillas, then a layer of the remaining pork mixture, then one more layer of tortillas. Spread the Salsa Verde evenly over the tortillas and top with the cheese. Place in the center of the preheated oven and bake for 30 to 40 minutes, until bubbly and slightly browned on top. Serve warm.

Winter

Winter

appetizers

salads

soups

vegetables & sides

entrees

desserts & pastries

Salsa Verde

MAKES ABOUT 1 QUART.

1 can tomatillas, drained
½ yellow onion, roughly chopped
1 poblano pepper, roughly
    chopped
2 cloves garlic

2 tablespoons cilantro, roughly
    chopped
Juice of 2 limes
½ teaspoon salt
1 fresh jalapeno pepper, seeded
    (optional)

Place everything in a blender and puree. Taste for seasoning. Refrigerate until
ready to use.

❋

Shrimp and Grits

*John and I have a strong connection to coastal Georgia and South Carolina. We were
engaged in Savannah, and made a baby (Sadie Anna) in Charleston. Plus my sister
has a house on Sea Island which we are lucky enough to visit now and then. I have
happily made it my job to taste as many versions of shrimp and grits as I can possibly
find. I'm sure that mine is not traditional—I never consulted a cookbook—but damn
if it's not good.*

SERVES 6.

4 tablespoons butter
4 ounces country ham, finely chopped
½ yellow onion, diced
1 teaspoon fresh chopped garlic
6 tablespoons flour
2 cups chicken stock, heated
2 cups shrimp or lobster stock, heated
1 cup heavy cream or milk

1 (14½-ounce) can chopped tomatoes, with
    juice
Salt and black pepper
1 tablespoon olive oil
36 large shrimp, peeled and deveined, tail on
Baked Cheese Grits (see page 76)
3 tablespoons roughly chopped flat leaf
    parsley

❋

Melt the butter with the country ham in a 2 to 3-quart sauce pan. Add the onion and cook over medium heat for 4 minutes. Add the garlic and cook 1 minute more. Stir in the flour to make a roux. Cook 1 minute, then whisk in the chicken stock, then the shrimp or lobster stock. Bring to a boil, stir in the cream or milk and tomato, and bring back to a boil. Reduce heat to low and simmer for 20 minutes. Taste for seasoning and add salt and pepper as you desire. Keep warm while you prepare the shrimp.

Season the shrimp lightly with salt and pepper. Heat the olive oil in a large sauté pan to just under smoking. Add the shrimp and cook over medium-high heat without turning for 3 minutes. Turn and cook 3 minutes more.

To serve, spoon Baked Cheese Grits into the center of 6 plates. Generously ladle the gravy over this and top with 6 shrimp per plate. Garnish with parsley and serve at once.

Winter

appetizers

salads

soups

vegetables & sides

entrees

desserts & pastries

Slow-Cooked Duck Legs with Dried Peaches and Bourbon

I was inspired to make this dish after Hellie, a fantastic cook in my supper club, prepared something similar one night and we all simply died over it. I talked about the dish for weeks. Hellie used figs and made a wonderful, intense brown sauce. I, of course had to make it Southern—hence the peaches and bourbon.

This is the way I find most folks prefer their duck: tender and moist and falling off the bone.

SERVES 6.

1 yellow onion, roughly chopped
6 cloves whole, peeled garlic
1 parsnip, peeled and roughly chopped
1 carrot, peeled and roughly chopped
6 duck leg quarters
Salt and black pepper to taste
6 fresh sage leaves (or ½ teaspoon dried)

3 sprigs fresh thyme (or ½ teaspoon dried)
2 cups red wine
2 cups chicken stock
12 dried peaches
½ cup bourbon

Preheat oven to 325°F. Place the onion, garlic, parsnip, and carrot into an oven-proof baking dish with a tightly-fitting lid. Place the duck legs on top. Season with salt and pepper and scatter the herbs on top. Pour the wine and stock around the duck, cover and place in the preheated oven. Cook for 1 hour, and check to see if it needs more liquid. If so, add equal parts of wine and stock. Cover again and cook another hour, until the legs are quite tender. Remove the legs and keep warm while you prepare the sauce.

While the legs are cooking, soak the dried peaches in the bourbon.

Discard the sage leaves and thyme stems, and place the remaining ingredients from the baking dish in a blender, and puree. You may have to do this in batches.

Pour the puree into a 2 to 3-quart sauce pan along with the peaches and bourbon. Bring to a simmer and taste for seasoning. I like to serve the duck with Pan-Seared Grits (see page 28), or mashed or roasted potatoes. Spoon the sauce over the duck legs and garnish with 2 of the peaches per serving.

Stewed Rabbit Hash
over Scallion Corn Pancakes

I made this stew for a wine tasting in the restaurant, to pair with a gutsy, peppery zinfandel, and may I modestly say, it was a huge success.

Happily, I have found the most wonderful local source for rabbit meat. The company is run by Mr. Grimm, and his motto is, "Break the habit, eat more rabbit." I think that's a fine idea.

SERVES 8 TO 10.

1 cup cider vinegar	3 cups chicken stock
½ cup Dijon mustard	1 yellow onion, chopped
2 pounds boneless rabbit pieces	2 teaspoons fresh chopped garlic
3 cups flour	2 carrots, peeled and sliced thinly
2 teaspoons salt	2 stalks celery sliced thinly
1 teaspoon black pepper	1 cup frozen green peas
3 tablespoons olive oil	Scallion Corn Pancakes (recipe follows)
1 cup red wine	

Whisk together the vinegar and mustard in a nonreactive bowl. Add the rabbit pieces and coat well. Let marinate at least 1 hour, or up to 3 hours.

Mix together the flour, salt, and pepper. Remove the rabbit from the marinade, shaking off excess, and dredge in the flour mixture.

Heat the oil in a large heavy pot or Dutch oven. Brown the rabbit on all sides, being careful not to crowd the pan. You may have to do this in batches. Remove the browned rabbit from the pan and deglaze with the red wine. Add the rabbit back to the pot, along with the stock and onion. Bring to a boil, turn heat to low, and simmer until the rabbit is tender, approximately 1 1/2 hours. Add the garlic, carrots, and celery to the pot and cook for 20 minutes more. Add the green peas, taste for seasoning, and serve over the Scallion Corn Pancakes.

❧

Scallion Corn Pancakes

To make the Scallion Corn Pancakes, follow the recipe for Fresh Corn Cakes (see page 110), omitting the corn, and making the pancakes approximately 4 inches in diameter.

❧

Braised Lamb Shanks with Sweet Potatoes and Mustard Greens

This is a real "beat the chill" kind of supper. The strong flavor of lamb is perfectly balanced by the mustard greens, and the sweet potatoes round it out.

An earthy wine from the Rhône is perfect with lamb shanks. I wish I had some of each right now!

SERVES 6.

6 lamb shanks
Salt and black pepper
3 tablespoons olive oil
1 yellow onion, chopped medium
1 tablespoon fresh chopped garlic
2 tablespoons tomato paste
2 (28-ounce cans) plum tomatoes, broken
    up, with their juice

2 cups dry red wine
6 packed cups mustard greens, cleaned
    and trimmed
3 sweet potatoes, peeled and cut into
    1-inch cubes
2 tablespoons vinegar-based pepper sauce

Preheat the oven to 435°F. Season the lamb shanks with salt and pepper, and place them in an 8-quart Dutch oven or other stove top, ovenproof cooking dish. Place in the preheated oven and cook for 20 minutes. Turn and cook 20 minutes more.

Remove the pan from the oven, pour off the fat and discard. Remove the shanks and keep warm. Place the pot over medium-high heat and add the olive oil. Heat and add the onion and garlic. Stir in the tomato paste, then the tomatoes, and wine. Add the shanks back to the pot. If the shanks are not covered with the tomatoes by at least two-thirds their volume, add water. Bring the mixture to a boil, turn to low, cover, and cook for 1 1/2 hours. Add the mustard greens and cook for 20 minutes. Add the sweet potatoes and cook 20 minutes more. Stir in the hot sauce, taste and adjust the seasoning.

Serve the shanks over steamed long grain rice, with the tomatoes, greens, and sweet potatoes spooned over and around.

Orange-Almond Pound Cake with Dark Fudge Sauce

appetizers

salads

soups

vegetables & sides

entrees

desserts & pastries

I believe I can say that this is my all-time favorite dessert. It's rustic and a little sophisticated all at the same time. Moist and rich, and not too sweet, and the combination of orange and chocolate is utterly divine.

SERVES 6 TO 8.

5 tablespoons unsalted butter, softened
⅓ cup mild olive oil
¾ cup sugar
1 tube (7 ounces) almond paste
Grated zest of 2 oranges

5 eggs
½ cup all-purpose flour
1 teaspoon baking powder
Dark Fudge Sauce (recipe follows)

Preheat the oven to 325°F. Butter and flour a 9-inch round cake pan. Line the bottom with wax or parchment paper.

Place the butter, olive oil, and sugar in the bowl of a mixer and beat until fluffy. Crumble the almond paste into the bowl and add the orange zest. Beat until smooth. Beat in the eggs. In a separate bowl, stir the flour and baking powder together. Mix this into the batter, and pour the batter into the prepared pan.

Bake for 45 minutes, or until a cake tester inserted into the middle of the cake comes out clean. Remove the cake from the oven and let it cool in the pan.

Invert the cake and place right side up on a platter. Serve with Dark Fudge Sauce.

Dark Fudge Sauce

MAKES ABOUT 3½ CUPS.

8 ounces semisweet chocolate chips
4 ounces unsweetened chocolate
1 cup light corn syrup
½ cup cream
2 tablespoons butter
1 teaspoon vanilla

Melt both kinds of chocolate with the corn syrup in the top of a double boiler. Mix well. Stir in the cream and butter. Remove from heat. Stir in the vanilla. Store covered in the refrigerator for up to 1 week. Microwave on high for 30 seconds before serving.

Chocolate Chèvre Cheesecake

I'm frequently tempted not to tell about the chèvre, because the idea turns some people off, and they would never know that it was there. What I do want them to know is that this cake has a depth and richness they've never had before. That's what the chèvre does.

MAKES 1 (8-INCH) CHEESECAKE.

(for the crust)
¼ cup chocolate wafer cookie crumbs
4 tablespoons unsalted butter, softened
2 tablespoons sugar

Preheat the oven to 350°F.

Place the cookie crumbs, butter, and sugar in the bowl of a food processor fitted with a steel blade. Process until you reach a spreading consistency. Remove from the processor and press into the bottom of a 9-inch springform pan. Set aside while you make the filling.

(for the filling)
1 pound cream cheese, at room
    temperature
½ pound mild, creamy chèvre, at room
    temperature
2 eggs
1 cup sugar

8 ounces semisweet chocolate, melted
2 tablespoons heavy cream
7 tablespoons strong black coffee
¾ cup sour cream
1 teaspoon grated orange zest
1 teaspoon bourbon

Put the cream cheese, chèvre, eggs, and sugar into the processor bowl and mix until smooth. Add the remaining ingredients and mix thoroughly. Pour the batter on top of the crust. Place the springform pan in the middle of a baking pan, and pour water into the pan to reach 1 inch up the sides of the springform pan.

Place in the center of the preheated oven and bake for 45 minutes. The cake will still be a little jiggly in the center, but will firm up as it cools. Remove the cake from the oven and let sit for 1 hour before refrigerating. Remove from the refrigerator 15 minutes before serving.

Serve with Cinnamon Scented Whipped Cream (recipe follows).

Winter

appetizers

salads

soups

vegetables & sides

entrees

desserts & pastries

❋

Cinnamon Scented Whipped Cream

MAKES ABOUT 1 QUART WHIPPED CREAM.

1 pint whipping cream
¼ cup confectioners' sugar
2 teaspoons ground cinnamon

Whip the cream in an electric mixer until soft peaks form. Add the sugar and cinnamon and whip 1 minute more. It should still be slightly soft, or "slumpy," as we like to say.

Winter

appetizers

salads

soups

vegetables & sides

entrees

desserts & pastries

Dried Cranberry and Chocolate Chip Cookies

We make a million of these between Thanksgiving and Christmas, but of course they're marvelous anytime of year. They're so pretty and festive, though. They just scream holiday.

MAKES ABOUT 5 DOZEN COOKIES.

1½ cups all-purpose flour	¾ cup granulated sugar
1 teaspoon baking soda	1 egg, beaten
½ teaspoon salt	1 teaspoon vanilla extract
1 teaspoon ground cinnamon	1½ cups rolled oats
1 cup unsalted butter	1 cup dried cranberries
½ cup firmly packed light brown sugar	1 cup white chocolate chips

Sift together the flour, baking soda, salt, and cinnamon. Set aside.

Cream together the butter and sugars until fluffy, then mix in the egg and vanilla. Mix in the flour mixture, then the oats. Stir in the dried cranberries and chocolate chips.

Cover and refrigerate for 1 hour.

Preheat the oven to 350°F. Spray a baking sheet with nonstick spray.

Place walnut-sized pieces of cookie dough on the prepared baking sheet, with at least 1 inch between cookies. Bake for 10 minutes. Allow to cool before removing from the cookie sheet. Store in an airtight container for up to 3 days.

Poached Pears with Caramel Sauce

This is a lovely winter dessert: understated and elegant.

SERVES 6.

appetizers

salads

soups

vegetables & sides

entrees

desserts & pastries

2½ cups red wine

2½ cups white wine

1½ cups sugar

1 cinnamon stick

1 wide strip of orange zest

6 firm, ripe pears

Caramel Sauce (recipe follows)

Bring the wine to a simmer with the sugar, cinnamon, and orange zest. Stir to dissolve the sugar.

While the wine is heating, peel the pears, slice in half lengthwise and use a small spoon to remove the core.

Place the pears in the simmering wine, cover and cook for 15 minutes. Remove from the heat and let the pears cool in the wine. Refrigerate until ready to use.

To serve, place 2 chilled pear halves in a sorbet bowl, and spoon the hot Caramel Sauce around them. Garnish with mint.

❋

Caramel Sauce

MAKES 1 QUART.

2 cups light brown sugar

2 cups cream

Stir the brown sugar and cream together in a 2-quart sauce pan. Place over medium heat and bring to a boil. Stir to dissolve all of the sugar. Let cool slightly before serving. You may make the sauce ahead of time and keep refrigerated until ready to use. Reheat in a microwave or double boiler.

❋

Red Velvet Cake with Cream Cheese Frosting

I don't know who decided that a chocolate cake should be red. Perhaps it could be made with beets, but you'll probably be relieved to know that we use food coloring instead. This is a delicious cake, and always a favorite.

Don't try to substitute butter for the margarine. It simply will not work.

MAKES 1 STANDARD 2-LAYER CAKE.

3½ cups flour
1 tablespoon baking soda
½ teaspoon salt
4 ounces unsweetened chocolate
2 teaspoons vanilla
2 cups sugar
1 cup brown sugar

1 cup margarine, softened
4 eggs, beaten
2½ cups buttermilk
¼ cup plus 1 tablespoon plus 1 teaspoon
    red food coloring
Cream Cheese Frosting (recipe follows)

Preheat the oven to 350°F. Grease and flour 2 (9-inch) round cake pans.

Sift together the flour, baking soda, and salt and set aside.

Melt the chocolate with the vanilla in the top of a double boiler. Let cool slightly.

Cream together the sugar, brown sugar, and margarine. Stir in the beaten eggs, then the chocolate.

Stir in the flour mixture, then the buttermilk, and food coloring. Divide evenly between the 2 pans. Place the pans on the center rack of the preheated oven, and bake for 30 minutes, or until a cake tester inserted into the cake comes out clean. Let the cakes cool in the pans for 20 minutes, then turn out on a rack and allow to cool completely before icing with Cream Cheese Frosting.

Cream Cheese Frosting

MAKES ENOUGH FROSTING FOR 1 (2-LAYER) CAKE.

8 ounces cream cheese, at room temperature
¼ cup sour cream
4 tablespoons unsalted butter, softened
1 cup confectioners' sugar
1 teaspoon vanilla

appetizers

salads

soups

vegetables & sides

entrees

desserts & pastries

Cream together the cream cheese, sour cream, and butter in
an electric mixer. Mix in the confectioners' sugar until smooth,
then mix in the vanilla. Spread evenly between the layers and over the room-
temperature cake. Refrigerate until serving.

Spring

Where we live in the upper South, spring is indeed a time of celebration. Our winters can be quite nasty, and, for some spiteful reason, winter seems to hit hardest right when you think it's almost over. So many years our tulip magnolias are frozen in full bud, along with apple and pear blossoms, and our spirits as well. Spring, like love, jilts us a few times, toying with our emotions. So when the earth really does begin to warm, humans seem to sprout on the lawns of parks and campuses like mushrooms in fairy circles, drawing nourishment from the grass and trees and sun. This time of year I can without prejudice state that there is not a more beautiful place on earth. It was on a visit at this time of year that I decided I had to move home to Nashville. As my plane flew lower and I began to see that indescribable green, as fresh and fragile as grasshopper wings, the green of the first spring leaves, then the pink blush of the redbud and the white drifts of dogwood trees throughout the rolling hills, I knew where I belonged.

When I was growing up we called the hills behind

49

our house fairyland. We packed picnics and dined among the violets and trout lilies. We waded in the cold creek and turned over rocks, searching for salamanders and tadpoles.

As I grew older, my celebrations became somewhat more sophisticated. Horse races and graduations, dance recitals and proms, then wedding parties and baby showers, my first opera, a christening—always a reason for a feast.

Springtime food can be a tricky dance. Our spirits call for light and fresh at a time when not much fresh is available yet. So we take thorough advantage of the good we can get—asparagus a thousand ways, carrots crunchy and bright, and sweet Vidalias just as soon as you can find them. Frequently I use seasoning to brighten the taste of winter's left over standbys: lemon, ginger, mint and dill all lend a lightness in keeping with a springtime mood. A giddy mood of second chances, new beginnings and possibilities galore. A cause for celebration.

Toasted Asparagus Sandwiches with Homemade Mayonnaise

Spring

This appetizer has been popular in Nashville since my Mama was little, but by the time I was a child, canned asparagus and store-bought mayo were the norm. We've brought freshness (and a little crunch) back to this classic hors d'oeuvre by blanching spring-harvest asparagus spears and slathering the bread with our garlicky Homemade Mayonnaise.

appetizers

salads

soups

vegetables & sides

entrees

desserts & pastries

SERVES 6 (2 SANDWICHES EACH).

12 spears (roughly 1 pound) fresh asparagus

6 slices thin-cut white or sourdough bread, crusts removed

½ cup Homemade Mayonnaise (recipe follows)

2 tablespoons melted butter

Cut away the bottom half of the asparagus. Heat a pot of salted water to a rapid boil. Drop in the trimmed asparagus and cook for 1 minute. Drain and cool in an ice-water bath. When completely cool, remove the asparagus and dry on tea or paper towels.

Liberally spread each slice of bread with Homemade Mayonnaise. Cut each slice of bread in half, into 2 triangles.

Roll up 1 asparagus spear in each bread triangle, pinching the end of the bread to seal.

Preheat oven to 375°F. Lightly grease a baking sheet. Place each rolled sandwich seam side down on the prepared baking sheet. Spread melted butter over the tops. Bake for approximately 10 minutes, until the bread is lightly toasted. Serve warm.

Spring

Homemade Mayonnaise

In my home and at Martha's, this is the Mother Sauce. Spread on every sandwich, mixed into deviled eggs, and dolloped on any fresh vegetable, a good Homemade Mayonnaise can change your life—or at least your outlook.

MAKES 3 1/2 CUPS.

2 whole eggs
2 egg yolks
Juice of 1 large lemon
2 teaspoons Dijon mustard
3 cloves garlic, minced
2 tablespoons flat leaf parsley,
    roughly chopped

1 teaspoon salt
½ teaspoon white pepper
½ teaspoon paprika
3 cups vegetable oil

Place all ingredients except the vegetable oil in the bowl of a food processor fitted with a steel blade.

Switch on the processor and, with the motor running, pour the vegetable oil through the feed tube in a slow, steady stream. The mixture should emulsify and thicken. Taste and adjust seasoning.

Keeps covered and refrigerated for up to 1 week.

Vidalia Onion Rings with Peanut Sauce

Spring

This dish combines the finest foods of south Georgia in one slightly newfangled bite.

Vidalias are mild and sweet, and the spicy, tangy Peanut Sauce is a perfect match. At Martha's, we pile the rings over lightly dressed salad greens, top them with the Peanut Sauce, some smoky bacon and crunchy roasted spring peas, and call it lunch! They're great for appetizers, too.

appetizers

salads

soups

vegetables & sides

entrees

desserts & pastries

SERVES 8.

3 Vidalia onions, cut into thin rings
2 cups buttermilk
Oil for frying
2 cups cornmeal
2 cups flour

1 teaspoon salt
½ teaspoon black pepper
Pinch cayenne
Oil for frying
1 cup Peanut Sauce (recipe follows)

Place the onion rings in a mixing bowl. Pour the buttermilk over the onion and let soak for at least 1 hour or overnight.

Heat oil in a fryer to 340°F. Mix the cornmeal, flour, and seasoning in a shallow pan or mixing bowl. Remove the onions from the buttermilk, shaking off any excess. Dredge in the flour mixture and shake off the excess. (At this point, you may place the onion rings on a tray, cover, and refrigerate for up to 3 hours before frying.) Fry until golden brown and crispy, about 5 minutes.

Serve with Peanut Sauce.

Peanut Sauce

This Asian-inspired Peanut Sauce is good on so many things—grilled chicken and pork, and Vidalia Onion Rings in particular.

MAKES 3 CUPS, SERVES ABOUT 12.

1 cup creamy peanut butter
¼ cup soy sauce
¼ cup seasoned rice wine
vinegar
1 tablespoon sesame oil
¼ cup brown sugar
2 cloves garlic, peeled and
minced

1 (1-inch) piece fresh ginger,
peeled and minced
Juice of 1 lime
1 tablespoon sambal oelek (Asian
chili sauce), optional
2 tablespoons water

Place all ingredients in the bowl of a food processor fitted with a steel blade. Mix thoroughly, taste, and adjust seasoning. Store covered and refrigerated for up to 1 week. Bring to room temperature before serving.

Watercress Tea Sandwiches

Spring

My friend Alice asked me to help her with a very pretty tea party in one of the beautiful old buildings on the historic Fisk University campus. Fisk, home of the Jubilee Singers and a jewel of an art collection, is experiencing a much-deserved renaissance. I was thrilled to be a part of the celebration. These sandwiches were Alice's favorite, so spring-y with a vibrant green hue and a nice little bite. Just like March.

This watercress butter would also be wonderful over steamed asparagus or pan-seared halibut.

MAKES 36 TEA SANDWICHES.

½ pound (2 sticks) butter, softened
1 bunch watercress, large stems removed,
    roughly chopped
2 teaspoons Dijon mustard

½ teaspoon salt
12 sandwich-size white bread slices,
    thin-cut
6 radishes, trimmed and shredded

Place the butter, watercress, Dijon mustard, and salt in the bowl of a food processor fitted with a steel blade. Process until smooth. Taste and adjust seasoning.

Use a 1 1/2-inch biscuit cutter to cut circles from the bread. (You should get 3 circles from each slice.)

Spread each circle with a liberal amount of the watercress mixture. Garnish with the shredded radish. Serve at room temperature.

Spring

Savory Bread Puddings with
Smoked Salmon, Red Onion, and Chèvre

I love to serve salmon in the spring—I think it's the pinkness of it all. I've made smoked salmon canapes for years, on a variety of breads, with all of sorts of spreads. After making these moist little puddings, however, I'm stuck on them. They're fine served at room temperature, or they will reheat nicely.

MAKES ABOUT 50 (1 1/2-INCH) "MINI" BREAD PUDDINGS.

2 tablespoons butter
½ red onion, sliced thinly
4 ounces thin-sliced smoked salmon, torn
    into small pieces
5 slices sourdough bread, cut in 1-inch
    cubes

½ cup soft chèvre
5 eggs
1 cup heavy cream
½ teaspoon salt
¼ teaspoon black pepper
1 teaspoon fresh dill or ½ teaspoon dried

Preheat oven to 375°F. Spray an 18 x 9-inch baking pan with nonstick spray.

Melt the butter in a sauté pan and cook the onion on medium-high heat for 5 minutes. Remove from heat and place the onion in a large mixing bowl, along with the salmon and bread cubes. Loosely crumble the chèvre into the bowl.

Beat the eggs and cream with the salt, pepper, and dill. Pour into the bowl and mix together well.

Pour the mixture into the prepared baking pan, making a 1 to 1 1/2-inch layer. Place in the center of the preheated oven and bake for approximately 20 minutes, until set. Remove from the oven and let cool before cutting. Serve warm.

Fried Soft-Shell Crab with Honey-Lime Vinaigrette

Spring

appetizers

salads

soups

vegetables & sides

entrees

desserts & pastries

A fresh soft-shelled crab tastes as briny and rich as the ocean itself, and spring is the only time you can get them—fresh, that is—and what a difference it makes! A fresh soft-shell crab is plump with juice. The slightly sweet and tart vinaigrette heightens the fresh flavor of the crab and balances its richness. This is a wonderful first course for 6, or serve 3 and make it an entree.

You may notice throughout the book that I soak almost everything I am going to fry in buttermilk. The acidity makes foods so tender, and it gives your final coating something good and thick to hold onto.

SERVES 6 (OR SERVES 3 AS AN ENTREE).

6 soft-shell crabs, cleaned
2 cups buttermilk
2 cups flour
2 cups cornmeal
1 teaspoon salt
½ teaspoon black pepper

Pinch cayenne
½ teaspoon garlic powder
Oil for frying
2 cups Honey-Lime Vinaigrette (recipe
   follows)

Place the cleaned soft-shell crabs in a mixing bowl and pour the buttermilk over them. Let soak at least 1 hour or up to 3.

In a shallow pan or bowl, mix together the flour, cornmeal, and seasoning. Remove the crabs from the buttermilk, shaking off any excess, and dredge in the flour mixture. Shake off the excess, and place on a baking sheet. Cover and refrigerate for at least 30 minutes, or up to 3 hours.

Heat the oil in a fryer or deep skillet to 340°F. Fry the soft-shells until golden brown, approximately 5 minutes. Drain well. Place on serving dishes or platter and pour the Honey-Lime Vinaigrette over the crabs. Serve immediately.

Spring

appetizers

salads

soups

vegetables & sides

entrees

desserts & pastries

Honey-Lime Vinaigrette

Another Asian-inspired sauce. I think that the fresh, clean flavors of many Asian foods match my springtime mood. This vinaigrette is wonderful with any seafood, or with fresh melon in the summer.

MAKES 2 CUPS, SERVES 8 TO 12.

½ cup honey

Juice of 2 limes

2 tablespoons soy sauce

2 tablespoons seasoned rice wine vinegar

2 cloves garlic, peeled and minced

1 tablespoon sambal oelek (Asian chili sauce), optional

1 tablespoon fresh mint, roughly chopped

1 cup vegetable oil

Place all ingredients in a blender and mix well.

Store covered and refrigerated for up to 1 week. Bring to room temperature before serving.

Martha's Chicken Salad

Spring

We probably make more of this than anything else in the restaurant. Consumption soars in the spring and as soon as the temperature rises above 65 degrees or so, any right-minded Southerner simply has to have a Chicken Salad sandwich and a glass of iced tea. It's been so long! Waiting through all those cold dreary months. Chicken Salad, of course, is not made simply for sandwiches. Plop a good scoop of it on a bed of greens, garnish it with some fruit and cheese straws, and you have the perfect ladies' lunch. In July we'll stuff our Martha's Chicken Salad in a tomato or avocado half for a nice, cool supper.

SERVES 6.

6 boneless, skinless chicken breasts
½ teaspoon salt
¼ teaspoon garlic powder
¼ teaspoon black pepper
¼ teaspoon Italian seasoning
Pinch cayenne

3 stalks of celery (including leaves), diced
2 tablespoons flat leaf parsley, roughly
    chopped
¼ cup mayonnaise
2 tablespoons sour cream
1 tablespoon Dijon mustard

Heat oven to 400°F. Place chicken breasts on a baking sheet and season with salt, garlic powder, black pepper, Italian seasoning and cayenne. Place baking sheet on the middle rack of the oven and roast for approximately 15 minutes, until just cooked through. Remove from the oven and allow chicken to cool. When cool enough to handle, cut away any fat or cartilage, then cut the chicken into 1/2-inch cubes.

In a large mixing bowl, combine the cooled, cubed chicken with the celery and parsley. Stir in the remaining ingredients. Taste and adjust seasoning. Refrigerate until ready to serve.

May be made up to 1 day ahead of time.

Spring

Tuna Salad with Capers and Dill

I eat Tuna Salad just about every day of my life. I'm a grazer, you see (owning a restaurant makes this easier for me than it is for most), and 'round about 10:00 A.M. I simply have to have a couple of spoonfuls of Tuna Salad. A protein craving, I believe. And, of course, we do make the best Tuna Salad I've ever had. Taste for yourself.

SERVES 6 TO 8.

3 (6-ounce) cans solid white tuna
2 ribs celery, finely diced
¼ small red onion, finely minced
½ cup mayonnaise
2 tablespoons Dijon mustard

Juice of 1 lemon
1 tablespoon capers
1 teaspoon fresh dill, minced (or
   ½ teaspoon dried)
Dash cayenne

Place the tuna in a fine colander and mash down on it to drain the tuna very, very well. Place the tuna in a mixing bowl and use a fork or your fingers to flake the tuna.

Add the remaining ingredients and mix well.

Egg Salad

Spring

*There are warm days in late spring when only Egg Salad will do.
I'll even make an Egg Salad sandwich for a breakfast on the go!
We use dill in ours, and a bit of Dijon mustard.*

MAKES 2 1/2 CUPS, SERVES ABOUT 6.

9 eggs
¼ small red onion, diced fine
1 tablespoon Dijon mustard
1½ tablespoons mayonnaise
¼ teaspoon salt

Dash white pepper
Dash cayenne
1 teaspoon fresh dill, minced
(or ½ teaspoon dried)

Place the eggs in a medium sauce pan and cover with water. Bring to a boil, uncovered, and let the eggs cook for 10 minutes. Drain the eggs, leaving them in the pot, then cover the eggs with ice water. Let them sit for 5 minutes, then peel and chop the eggs, and place them in a mixing bowl.

Add the remaining ingredients and mix well. Taste to adjust seasoning.

Spring

Baby Spinach and Pan Seared Salmon with Grapefruit, Avocado, and Hearts of Palm

We prepared this salad for a huge ladies' luncheon in the Carriage House at the Plantation. It was a beautiful spring day, with about 200 beautiful ladies drinking wine and eating salad. Everyone wanted to linger and bask in it all.

SERVES 8.

1 tablespoon olive oil	2 cups grapefruit segments
8 (4-ounce) salmon fillets	2 avocados, cut into thin wedges
Salt and pepper	and peeled
1 bag baby spinach	1 cup crumbled feta cheese
8 ounces Lemon-Thyme	
Vinaigrette (see page 85)	

Preheat the oven to 400°F. Heat the olive oil over medium-high heat. Season the salmon with salt and pepper, add to the pan, and cook without turning for 4 minutes. Turn the salmon over and place the skillet in the preheated oven to bake. Cook another 4 minutes for slightly medium-rare fish, or to desired doneness. Keep warm while you prepare the salad.

Toss the spinach with the Lemon-Thyme Vinaigrette in a large salad bowl. Arrange the remaining ingredients over the spinach and top with the salmon.

Cracked Wheat Salad

This salad is a bit unusual, and one of my very favorites. The beets are an addition to the original plan. They turn the salad a very spring-y shade of pink, add some good crunch and lots of minerals, too.

Spring

appetizers

salads

soups

vegetables & sides

entrees

desserts & pastries

SERVES 6.

2 cups cracked wheat
Juice of 4 lemons
¼ cup olive oil
1 cucumber, peeled and shredded
1 (4-ounce) bag radishes, trimmed and
   shredded
1 medium carrot, peeled and shredded
1 medium beet, peeled and shredded

1 clove garlic, peeled
   and minced
2 tablespoons flat leaf
   parsley, roughly chopped
2 tablespoons mint, roughly chopped
2 tablespoons cilantro, roughly chopped
2 teaspoons salt
½ teaspoon black pepper

Place the cracked wheat in a mixing bowl and stir in the lemon juice and olive oil. Cover with plastic wrap and refrigerate at least 2 hours, or overnight.

    Add the remaining ingredients and mix well. Taste and adjust seasoning.

Crispy Iceberg Wedge

Martha's Crispy Iceberg Wedge can boast many stalwart fans, not the least of which is my sister Sallie. She never orders anything else! She (and many others) just can't work beyond the wedge. That poor iceberg lettuce which drew so much disfavor in the eighties is back in fashion again, although for some (like Sallie) it never went out of style. We like to douse ours in our garlicky Buttermilk Blue Cheese Dressing and serve a scoop of "main course salad"—tuna, chicken, egg, or shrimp—on the side. Here's the basic formula, followed by particulars of the fixin's.

SERVES 4.

1 head iceberg lettuce
4 pieces cooked bacon, crumbled
4 hard-boiled eggs, peeled and roughly
    chopped
2 cups Sourdough Croutons (recipe follows)

1 cup Dania's Honduran Pickled Vegetables
    (recipe follows)
8 ounces Blue Cheese Buttermilk Dressing
    (recipe follows)

Trim lettuce of any wilty leaves, and cut into 4 wedges. Place each wedge on a separate plate and garnish with an equal amount of the remaining ingredients. Serve immediately.

Sourdough Croutons

I think that what makes these so good is the marvelous sourdough bread we use—baked at Provence, an artisanal bakery here in Nashville. We frequently use these to garnish soups as well as salads.

SERVES 6 TO 8.

4 slices sourdough bread, cut into 1-inch cubes
2 tablespoons olive oil
Pinch of each: salt, black pepper, garlic powder

Preheat oven to 325°F.

In a mixing bowl, toss the bread cubes with the remaining ingredients. Spread out on an ungreased baking sheet and bake for fifteen minutes, tossing once, until toasted through.

Let cool, then store in an airtight container for up to 3 days.

Dania's Honduran Pickled Vegetables

MAKES 3 QUARTS.

Many gifts have come my way, but few as dear as the gift of knowing Dania. She was our first kitchen employee who wasn't already a long-standing friend, and when she first came to us, she spoke barely any English at all. Her radiant smile and soft brown eyes said enough, and her amazing work ethic inspired us all. Not to mention her impeccable palate—Dania is the only person I know who can recreate any dish after tasting it only once.

One more thing for which I am truly grateful is her delicious recipe for Dania's Honduran Pickled Vegetables. They not only top our Crispy Iceberg Wedge, but garnish every cold plate at Martha's. Dania first served them to us atop her homemade Christmas tamales—such a gift! I eat them straight, like candy, and highly recommend them in a martini. The pinkish hue and slight sweetness from the beets makes a springtime view only rosier.

1 cup trimmed green beans
1 poblano pepper, cored and seeded, cut in strips
9 stalks celery, cut in 2-inch strips
2 red onions, cut in strips
5 carrots, cut in ¼-inch circles
3 medium beets, peeled and cut in ¼-inch thick circles
¾ cup sugar

2 teaspoons salt
1 tablespoon black peppercorns
1 tablespoon red pepper flakes
5 bay leaves
1 pint water
½ cup tarragon vinegar
4 green onions, trimmed and cut in thirds, lengthwise

Bring a large pot of water to boil. Turn off the heat and add the green beans, poblano pepper, celery, red onion, and carrots. Let stand for 5 minutes. Drain and place the vegetables in a large mixing bowl.

In a smaller pot, place the beets with the sugar, salt, peppers, bay leaves, and pint of water. Bring the mixture to a boil and cook for 5 minutes. Pour the mixture over the reserved vegetables.

Add the vinegar, green onions, and additional water as needed to cover the vegetables. Let cool, cover and refrigerate for up to 2 weeks.

Blue Cheese Buttermilk Dressing

Spring

appetizers

salads

soups

vegetables & sides

entrees

desserts & pastries

Thicken this dressing up a bit and it's a fabulous dip for veggies—particularly blanched asparagus. They're on the menu at all of our spring parties.

SERVES 8 TO 12.

1 cup crumbled blue cheese
½ cup mayonnaise
½ cup sour cream
½ cup buttermilk

2 cloves garlic, peeled and
   minced
¼ teaspoon cayenne

Place all the ingredients in a blender and mix well.
   Store covered and refrigerated for up to 1 week.

Shrimp Salad

Ladies love a Shrimp Salad. I know this because I am one. Martha's Shrimp Salad is particularly tasty, with a bit of a zip and a lovely celery-filled crunch.

SERVES 6 TO 8.

2 pounds cooked large shrimp, peeled and
   deveined, tail off
½ cup mayonnaise
½ cup sour cream
2 tablespoons Dijon mustard
2 tablespoons capers, with a bit of the juice

½ small red onion, minced
3 stalks celery with leaves, diced small
1 tablespoon flat leaf parsley, roughly
   chopped
Juice and zest of 2 lemons
Salt and cayenne, to taste

Chop shrimp into bite-sized pieces. Place in a large bowl with remaining ingredients and mix well. Taste and adjust seasoning.

Spring

Ginger-Lime Broth with Shrimp and Asparagus

I first made this soup for Valentine's supper. The pink of the shrimp and the pale green asparagus make a visibly stunning appetizer. The broth is invigorating and light—a good way to start out any spring evening, particularly a night meant for love.

SERVES 6.

6 cups shrimp or lobster stock
¼ pound fresh ginger, roughly chopped
½ cup seasoned rice wine vinegar
Juice of 3 limes
¼ cup soy sauce
½ cup brown sugar
1 tablespoon sambal oelek (Asian chili sauce), optional
1 tablespoon vegetable oil
1 small red onion, halved and thinly sliced

4 cloves garlic, peeled and minced
1 medium carrot, peeled and cut into match sticks
2 stalks celery, thinly sliced
1 bunch asparagus, cut in ½-inch rounds
½ cup frozen green peas
18 large shrimp, cooked, peeled, and deveined, tail off
1 bunch fresh mint, picked and roughly chopped

In a large pot, heat the shrimp or lobster stock with the ginger to a simmer. Simmer for twenty minutes, then drain into another pot, discarding ginger.

Add the vinegar, lime juice, soy sauce, brown sugar, and sambal oelek (optional) to the stock. Keep warm.

Heat the vegetable oil in a sauté pan. Add the onion and cook 2 minutes, then add the garlic, carrot, and celery. Cook 2 minutes more, then add to the stock. Bring the stock to a simmer and add the asparagus and peas.

Slice the shrimp in half, lengthwise.

Ladle the stock with vegetables into serving bowls. Add 6 pieces of shrimp and garnish with the mint. Serve hot.

Saffron Carrot Bisque with Spring Pesto

This is one of my favorite soups—heady with saffron and peppery with fresh pesto. Think about the carrot base as a possible sauce for shrimp or a light white fish.

SERVES 6.

appetizers

salads

soups

vegetables & sides

entrees

desserts & pastries

4 tablespoons butter
4 medium carrots, peeled and cut into thin circles
1 small red onion, roughly chopped
2 cloves garlic, peeled and minced
3 cups chicken stock
Pinch saffron

1 cup orange juice
2 tablespoons honey
Salt and white pepper to taste
Sourdough Croutons (see page 65)
Spring Pesto (recipe follows)

Melt the butter in a large sauce pan. Add the carrots, onion, and garlic and cook for 5 minutes. Add the stock and saffron and bring to a boil. Turn to simmer and cook until the carrots are completely softened, approximately 10 minutes. Remove from heat and cool slightly.

In batches, place all of the ingredients of the sauce pan into a blender and mix thoroughly, adding orange juice to thin.

Stir in the honey, and season to taste with salt and white pepper.

Serve warm with Sourdough Croutons and Spring Pesto.

Spring Pesto

I am a bit handicapped as a chef, because pesto always seems like the perfect answer to me. I spoon it into soups, slather over chicken, pork, fish, and beef, and spread it on sandwiches instead of mayo. I love it in this thick, creamy soup, but also use it for a brothy soup such as chicken and rice or vegetable.

This is actually a cross between gremolata and pesto. We make this in the late spring, before the basil is in season. A combination of any tender-leafed herb is fine.

MAKES ABOUT 2 QUARTS.

1 bunch flat leaf parsley, stemmed
1 bunch cilantro, stemmed
1 bunch mint, stemmed
1½ cups feta cheese
1½ cups Parmesan cheese
5 cloves garlic, minced and roughly
   chopped

3 tablespoons capers
Juice and zest of 3 lemons
2 teaspoons red pepper flakes
2 cups olive oil

Place all the fresh herbs in a mixing bowl and toss.

Place half of the mixed herbs in the bowl of a food processor fitted with a steel blade. Add half of the remaining ingredients and process to a rough textured paste. Place prepared pesto into a storage container, re-attach bowl and blade and repeat. Store covered and refrigerated for up to 1 week. Mix thoroughly before serving.

Creamy Vidalia Onion Soup
with Thyme and Chèvre

Spring

A Southern version of the French classic: ours is made with Georgia onions and Alabama goat cheese (chèvre).

SERVES 6.

4 tablespoons butter
4 Vidalia onions, roughly chopped
8 cups beef stock
1 cup red wine
6 sprigs fresh thyme

2 tablespoons honey
Salt and white pepper
   to taste
8 ounces soft chèvre

Melt the butter in a large sauté pan. Add the Vidalia onion with a pinch of salt and cook slowly until very soft, approximately 30 minutes.

Heat the stock with the wine and thyme to a boil. Simmer for 20 minutes.

In a blender in batches, puree the Vidalias with the beef stock and thyme. Stir in the honey and season to taste with salt and white pepper. Serve warm with a small scoop of soft chèvre.

Roasted Chicken Soup with Orzo and Lemon

This soup makes Georgette clap her hands. Our beautiful, charming, and all-around-amazing general manager is of distinct Mediterranean heritage. Lemon and garlic are home-cooking ingredients to her.

If you like, you can grill the chicken instead of roasting. It brings in the essence of light smoke.

SERVES 6 TO 8.

4 boneless, skinless chicken breasts
2 tablespoons plus 2 tablespoons olive oil
½ teaspoon salt
¼ teaspoon black pepper
½ medium red onion, sliced thinly
3 cloves garlic, peeled and minced
1 carrot, peeled and sliced thinly
2 stalks celery, sliced thinly
Pinch salt and pepper

¼ teaspoon cayenne
½ teaspoon dried oregano
8 cups chicken stock, heated
Juice of 3 lemons
1 cup orzo pasta, cooked by package
    instructions, drained and cooled
6 tablespoons grated Parmesan cheese
1 bunch flat leaf parsley, roughly chopped

Preheat oven to 400°F. Rinse the chicken breasts and pat dry. Place the breasts on a baking sheet, drizzle with 2 tablespoons olive oil, and season with salt and pepper. Place in the preheated oven and roast for twelve minutes. Set aside to cool.

Heat remaining olive oil in a large sauce pan. Add onion and cook for 2 minutes. Add garlic, carrot, celery, salt, pepper, cayenne, and dried oregano. Cook another 5 minutes, then pour in the chicken stock. Bring to a boil, turn to simmer and cook 30 minutes.

When chicken is cool enough to handle, shred into small bite-sized pieces. Add chicken and the lemon juice to the soup for last 5 minutes of simmering.

To serve, spoon a little cooked orzo into serving bowls, ladle soup over the orzo, then garnish with Parmesan cheese and parsley.

Spring Pea Soup with Heavy Cream and Carrot Puree

Spring

appetizers

salads

soups

vegetables & sides

entrees

desserts & pastries

This is a luncheon-y soup: something I would serve with a good salad for a wonderful early spring meeting. The carrots are a must to give it all a zip—to both the eye and the tooth.

SERVES 6.

3 tablespoons plus 1 tablespoon butter
1 bunch scallions, white and green parts,
   roughly chopped
8 cups chicken stock, heated
1 (16-ounce package) frozen baby green
   peas, thawed
2 tablespoons seasoned rice wine vinegar
Salt and pepper to taste

1 medium carrot,
   peeled and cut
   into thin circles
¼ cup water
2 tablespoons brown sugar
Juice of 1 lemon
1 half-pint heavy cream, whipped to soft
   peaks

Melt 3 tablespoons of butter in a large sauce pan. Add the scallions and cook for 5 minutes. Pour in the stock and bring to a boil. Add the peas and cook until tender, approximately 7 minutes. Remove from the heat and let cool slightly. In a blender, puree in batches. Add the rice wine vinegar and salt and pepper to taste. Keep warm.

Melt the remaining butter in a sauce pan. Add the carrot and a pinch of salt and cook for 5 minutes. Add the water, brown sugar, and the lemon. Stir and cook until carrot is completely soft. Remove from heat and puree in a blender.

To serve, ladle the pea soup into serving bowls. Garnish with a spoonful of whipped cream and a little of the carrot puree.

Baked Spinach and Artichoke Hearts

Economy and common sense have moved me to use frozen spinach and canned artichoke hearts in this truly marvelous casserole, so you can make it any time of year. But it does give a nod to two of springtime's earliest crops. I love it with a juicy Roasted Boneless Leg of Lamb with Watercress Pesto (see page 88).

SERVES 10 TO 14.

1 tablespoon olive oil
½ red onion, sliced thinly
½ teaspoon Italian seasoning
3 cloves garlic, minced
1 (10-ounce) box chopped frozen
    spinach, thawed and
    squeezed dry
1 (15-ounce) can quartered
    artichoke hearts
6 pieces sourdough bread, cut
    into 1-inch cubes

6 eggs, beaten
3 cups heavy cream
1 teaspoon salt
½ teaspoon white pepper
Juice of 1 lemon
1 cup creamy chèvre
¾ plus ¼ cup grated Parmesan
    cheese

Preheat oven to 350°F.

Heat olive oil in a sauté pan. Add onion and Italian seasoning and cook 5 minutes. Add garlic and cook 1 minute more. Remove from heat and place in a large mixing bowl. Add the spinach, artichoke hearts, and bread cubes and toss. In a separate bowl, stir together the eggs and cream with the salt, pepper, and lemon juice. Mix into the casserole, along with the chèvre and 3/4 cup grated Parmesan. Pour the mixture into a baking dish and top with the 1/4 cup grated Parmesan. Cover with foil and bake for 45 minutes. Remove foil and bake another 15 minutes, until nicely browned and puffed through.

Almond Rice Pilaf

SERVES 6 TO 8.

1 tablespoon olive oil
½ red onion, minced
2 cups Basmati or long grain rice
4 cups chicken stock, heated
1 bay leaf
½ teaspoon salt
¼ teaspoon white pepper
1 cup toasted almonds

1 cup frozen green
   peas, thawed
2 tablespoons flat leaf
   parsley, roughly
   chopped
Juice of 1 lemon

appetizers

salads

soups

vegetables & sides

entrees

desserts & pastries

Preheat the oven to 350°F. Heat the oil in a sauce pan. Add the onion and cook for 5 minutes. Add the rice and cook, stirring, until lightly browned, approximately 5 minutes. Add the chicken stock, bay leaf, salt, and white pepper. Stir and bring to a boil. Stir very well, place a lid on top and place in the preheated oven for 20 minutes. Remove from oven, turn out on a sheet pan and let cool slightly. Lightly mix in the almonds, peas, parsley, and lemon juice. Serve warm.

Spring

Baked Cheese Grits

I cannot imagine anything more comforting than a spoonful of our fresh-out-of-the-oven Baked Cheese Grits. The texture is rich like a custard, and we never skimp on yummy Parmesan cheese!

We serve these Cheese Grits all year long, but I think I like them best in the spring as a fluffy base for Chicken Croquettes with Creamed Mushrooms (see page 80).

SERVES 5 TO 6.

2 cups cream	2 cups Parmesan cheese,
2 cups water	shredded
1 teaspoon salt	½ cup buttermilk
½ teaspoon white pepper	2 eggs, beaten
1 cup yellow grits or polenta	½ teaspoon granulated garlic

Preheat oven to 350°F. Grease a 2-quart baking dish.

In a medium sauce pan, bring the cream and water to a boil with the salt and white pepper. Add the grits or polenta, whisking. Cook over medium heat until thickened. Remove from the heat and add the cheese, mixing well to a smooth, creamy consistency. Add the buttermilk, then the eggs and mix well.

Pour into the baking dish and place in the center of the preheated oven. Bake until puffed and golden brown, approximately 30 minutes.

Saffron Couscous with Golden Raisins

One of my greatest culinary compliments came when a Kurdish friend with whom I worked told me my Saffron Couscous tasted just like his mama's. I was so proud. As with most cities in the southeast, Nashville has only recently become the melting pot which so many other American cities have been for so long. I embrace and celebrate this cultural diversity. I believe you can learn a lot about a person's culture through tasting what they eat. Having tasted couscous in many forms, I know I want to learn more about all of the Middle East.

This version is wonderful either warm or at room temperature. We like to serve it in the springtime as a side for our Seared Halibut with Lemon-Thyme Vinaigrette (see page 85).

SERVES 6 TO 8.

1½ cups instant couscous
¼ cup olive oil
1½ cups water
1 teaspoon salt
Pinch saffron
Grated zest and juice of 3 lemons
½ teaspoon cinnamon

1 teaspoon ground cumin
¼ teaspoon cayenne
½ cup toasted sliced almonds
¼ cup golden raisins
3 green onions, white and green parts, sliced thinly
2 tablespoons mint, roughly chopped

Place the couscous in a mixing bowl, along with the olive oil. In a sauce pan, bring the water to a boil with the salt and saffron and pour over the couscous. Cover with plastic wrap and allow to steam for 5 minutes.

Remove wrap and fluff with a fork. Allow the couscous to cool completely, fluffing occasionally, before adding remaining ingredients and mixing well.

Serve warm or room temperature. Reheat in the oven or microwave.

Roasted Spring Vegetables in Warm Vinaigrette

I first made these for a class I taught at the Viking Culinary Center in Franklin, Tennessee. It makes a very elegant but simple first course for a fancy dinner party. Spring onions are the earliest bulbs, usually sold with the greens still attached. Leeks would be good, as well.

SERVES 6 TO 8.

1 bunch spring onions, white parts only, trimmed and thinly sliced

2 carrots, peeled and cut into match sticks

1 cup shiitake (or button) mushroom caps

A bit plus 4 tablespoons good olive oil

Salt and white pepper to taste

1 bunch asparagus, trimmed and sliced in half lengthwise

2 cloves garlic

3 tablespoons champagne vinegar

Pinch sugar

Preheat oven to 425°F. Toss the onions in a bowl with the carrots, shiitakes, a bit of olive oil, salt and white pepper. Spread on a sheet pan and roast in the oven for 15 minutes. Add the asparagus stalks and toss then roast another 10 minutes. Remove from the oven and place in a mixing bowl.

Heat the 4 tablespoons olive oil in a sauté pan. Add the garlic and lightly sauté. Do not brown. Pour in the vinegar (careful, it may spatter), then stir in sugar and salt and pepper to taste. Pour the vinaigrette over the vegetables and serve warm.

Carrot Potato Puree

I can't get enough of the taste of carrots with saffron. The sweet sultriness is intoxicating. I particularly love this dish with Red Snapper in Fennel Broth (see page 84), but it's also great with a simple roasted chicken.

Spring

appetizers

salads

soups

vegetables & sides

entrees

desserts & pastries

SERVES 6 TO 8.

1 pound carrots, peeled and roughly chopped
1 pound yellow skin potatoes
½ pound butter
Pinch saffron threads
2 teaspoons salt
¼ teaspoon cayenne pepper

Place the carrots and potatoes in separate pots and cover each with salted water. Place each over high heat and bring to a boil. Cook until quite tender, approximately 20 minutes. Drain in separate colanders. Pull the peel away from the potatoes and discard. Place the potatoes in a mixing bowl, along with carrots and remaining ingredients. Mash very well, or press through a food mill. Taste and adjust seasoning. Serve warm.

Chicken Croquettes with Creamed Mushrooms

This is what I cooked one fine spring day when the Food Network's The Best Of came to pay Martha's a visit. It is also what my mother prepared for every birthday, graduation, or other special event. This is my version of a recipe I found written in precise penmanship in the 1864 journal of my great-great-Aunt Kate. From a dietetic point of view, croquettes are about as in keeping with the times as creamed chipped beef. None of my customers seem to mind.

SERVES 6 TO 8.

3 pounds boneless, skinless chicken
    breasts, rinsed and patted dry
½ teaspoon salt
¼ teaspoon black pepper
¼ teaspoon dry thyme leaves
Pinch cayenne
8 tablespoons butter
3 stalks celery, finely chopped
½ red onion, finely chopped

2 cloves garlic, minced
½ cups flour
1 cup milk, heated
2 tablespoons flat leaf parsley, roughly
    chopped
4 cups dry, unseasoned bread crumbs
Vegetable oil for frying
Creamed Mushrooms (recipe follows)

Preheat the oven to 400°F. Place chicken breasts on a baking sheet and season with salt, black pepper, dry thyme leaves, and cayenne. Place baking sheet on middle rack of oven and bake for approximately 15 minutes, until just cooked through. Remove the pan from the oven and let the chicken cool while you prepare the sauce.

Melt the butter in a sauce pan on medium-high heat. Add celery and onion along with a pinch of salt and pepper and cook until soft, approximately 3 minutes. Add garlic and cook 1 minute more. Add flour and stir to coat vegetables well. Cook, stirring often, for 3 more minutes. Slowly whisk in milk. After milk is incorporated, simmer the sauce at least 10 minutes, whisking often. Taste for seasoning and adjust with salt and pepper as needed.

Cut cooled chicken into large pieces, place in the food processor and pulse until finely chopped. Place the chopped chicken in a mixing bowl along with the sauce. Add parsley and mix thoroughly. Cover and refrigerate for 1 hour. Form chicken mixture into golf ball-sized balls then roll in bread crumbs. Refrigerate the croquettes for at least 30 minutes.

Heat vegetable oil in a deep fryer to 350°F. Fry croquettes for 5 to 10 minutes, until golden brown. Drain and serve with Creamed Mushrooms.

Croquettes may be formed and refrigerated for at least 1 day before frying. They may be fried up to 3 hours before serving, then placed on a baking sheet and heated uncovered for 15 minutes in a 375°F oven.

Creamed Mushrooms

MAKES ABOUT 3 CUPS.

4 tablespoons butter
½ medium red onion, minced
Pinch each: salt, pepper, dry thyme leaves
1 clove garlic, minced
2 scallions, thinly sliced
Dash sherry
4 tablespoons flour

1 cup milk, heated
1 pound button mushrooms, thinly sliced
1 teaspoon flat leaf parsley, roughly
　　chopped

Heat the butter in a sauté pan on medium-high heat. Add the onion, salt, pepper, and dry thyme leaves and cook until transparent, approximately 3 minutes. Add garlic and scallions and cook 1 minute more. Splash the pan with a bit of sherry and cook until the liquid evaporates. Stir in flour and cook 1 minute. Slowly whisk in milk. Add mushrooms, stir, and cook for 20 minutes. Remove the pan from heat and stir in the parsley. Season to taste with salt and pepper.

The sauce may be made at least 1 day ahead of time and slowly reheated on low heat.

Chicken Potpie with Spring Vegetables

I love to make (and eat) potpie, a dish in which every flavor and texture is married in a steamy bliss under a crispy brown crust. I make them most of the year, but this version takes advantage of tender spring vegetables.

MAKES 2 PIES, SERVES ABOUT 8.

(to cook the chicken)	3 bay leaves
1 whole fryer chicken	1 tablespoon salt
1 onion, roughly chopped	1 teaspoon black peppercorns
2 carrots, roughly chopped	3 sprigs of fresh thyme,
2 stalks celery, roughly chopped	or ½ teaspoon dried

Remove the neck bone and giblets from the cavity of the chicken. Discard or save for another use. Rinse the chicken well, inside and out.

Place the chicken in a large pot along with the remaining ingredients. Cover with cold water and place the pot over high heat. Bring the water to a boil, reduce heat to simmer, and cook for 1 hour, skimming off the scum that rises to the surface.

Remove the pot from the heat. Remove the chicken from the pot and place in a colander in the sink to allow it to cool. When the chicken is cool enough, remove the skin and pull the meat from the bones. Tear the meat into bite-sized pieces and set aside.

Refrigerate the pot with the broth in it while you prepare the filling for the pie, or overnight.

When the broth is cold, remove the fat from the top and drain off the vegetables, reserving the broth.

(for the filling)	1 quart chicken broth, heated
8 ounces butter	1 bunch asparagus, trimmed and sliced into
1 onion, diced medium	½-inch pieces
2 carrots, peeled and diced medium	½ pound button mushrooms, halved
Heart and leaves from 1 bunch celery, diced	¼ cup frozen green peas
medium	Salt and pepper to taste
4 tablespoons flour	1 tablespoon parsley, chopped

In a large sauté pan or Dutch oven, melt the butter. Add the onion and cook for 3 minutes, until wilted. Add the carrots and celery and cook 5 minutes more. Stir in the flour and cook about 2 or 3 minutes, stirring. Whisk in half of the hot broth, bring to a simmer, then pour in the other half. Bring to a simmer and cook on low heat for 10 minutes. Add asparagus, mushrooms, peas, and reserved chicken meat. Combine well and taste for seasoning. Stir in chopped parsley, then pour into 2 (9-inch) pie pans or 1 (18 x 9-inch) Pyrex or other baking dish.

appetizers

salads

soups

vegetables & sides

entrees

desserts & pastries

Set aside while you prepare the cornmeal crust.

(for the cornmeal crust)
2 cups all-purpose flour
1 cup yellow cornmeal
2 teaspoons salt
4 tablespoons cold butter, cut into bits

4 tablespoons shortening
8 to 12 tablespoons ice water
1 egg yolk
2 tablespoons milk

Place the flour, cornmeal, and salt in the bowl of a food processor fitted with a steel blade. Pulse to combine. Add the butter and pulse until the butter is the size of tiny gravel. Add the shortening and pulse to combine. Turn the motor on and add the ice water in bits until you have a shaggy dough that will just hold together.

Gather the dough and divide into 2 balls. Cover and refrigerate for 5 minutes before rolling out the dough.

Preheat the oven to 375°F. Roll dough to 1/8 of an inch. Roll the dough onto your rolling pin, then drape over the filled pie pan or baking dish. Crimp the edges.

Beat together the egg yolk and milk to make an egg wash. Use a pastry brush to apply egg wash to the crust. Cut a few slits in the pastry to vent the steam. Place in the center of the preheated oven and bake for 20 minutes, until the pastry is golden brown and the filling is bubbly hot.

Remove from the oven and let rest 5 minutes before serving.

Red Snapper in Fennel Broth

I know a lot of people claim to dislike the licoricey taste of fennel. I think that it does taste unusual at first, but I have won many a convert with this little dish. The broth is so fresh-tasting and light, but comforting as well—a titillating little meal.

SERVES 6.

2 tablespoons plus 2 tablespoons
    olive oil
1 bulb fennel, sliced thinly
1 red onion, sliced thinly
1 stalk celery, sliced thinly
3 cloves garlic, peeled and
    minced
1 (28-ounce) can chopped
    tomatoes, with juice

4 tablespoons dry white wine
2 cups fish or shrimp stock
Juice of 1 lemon
6 (6-ounce) snapper fillets
Salt and pepper to taste
Carrot and Potato Puree (see
    page 79)
3 tablespoons flat leaf parsley,
    roughly chopped

Heat 2 tablespoons olive oil in a sauté pan. Add the fennel, red onion, and celery and sauté for about 5 minutes. Add the garlic and cook 1 minute more. Add the tomato and white wine and heat through. Add the stock and bring to a simmer. Add the lemon juice, taste for seasoning, and keep warm.

Preheat oven to 425°F. Season the snapper with salt and pepper. Heat remaining olive oil in a separate sauté pan. Sear the fish, cut side down, in the hot oil, getting a nice, crispy brown crust. Turn and briefly cook, then add the broth. Bring to a simmer then place in the hot oven for 5 minutes. We serve the fish in a soup dish over a scoop of Carrot and Potato Puree and garnish it with chopped flat leaf parsley.

Seared Halibut with Lemon-Thyme Vinaigrette

Spring

appetizers

salads

soups

vegetables & sides

entrees

desserts & pastries

This is our most popular dinner plate. Something about all of the tastes and textures combine into a simply sublime meal. Spring's the season for halibut. It's really reasonably priced—and so white and flaky. A good choice for those who might be leery of fishier fish. We actually served this at a banquet for 375 guests. Was I nervous? Ask John.

SERVES 6.

1 tablespoon olive oil
6 (6-ounce) halibut fillets

Salt and white pepper to taste
Lemon-Thyme Vinaigrette (recipe follows)

Preheat oven to 400°F. Heat a nonstick pan with 1 tablespoon olive oil to just under smoking. Season each fillet with salt and pepper. Sear, cut side down, getting a brown and crispy crust. Cook without turning for 4 minutes. Turn and cook 1 minute more. Place in the preheated oven until fillets are cooked through, approximately 5 minutes. Don't overcook or the fish will dry out.

We serve the halibut over warmed couscous and top it with Lemon-Thyme Vinaigrette.

✤ Lemon-Thyme Vinaigrette

This is actually our "house" vinaigrette. We toss it with field greens for our simplest salad. Here, it's the perfect finish for this delicate, light fish.
MAKES ABOUT 4 CUPS.

Juice and zest of 4 lemons
½ cup rice wine vinegar
2 teaspoons Dijon mustard
3 cups olive oil
1 tablespoon fresh thyme leaves
2 tablespoons honey
½ teaspoon salt
½ teaspoon white pepper

Place all of the ingredients in a blender and whir to emulsify.

✤

Spring

Herb Roasted Pork Loin with Rhubarb Chutney

appetizers

salads

soups

vegetables & sides

entrees

desserts & pastries

This is the perfect thing to feed a small crowd, say, for Easter brunch or a day at the races. The properly cooked roast is so juicy and flavorful. I like to slice it thinly and serve it on a platter for stuffing into biscuits or rolls. Remember that pork loins are large! A whole loin will easily feed 15 to 20 adults. You can freeze 1/2 before cooking, or, if you have any leftovers, it's divine the next day!

SERVES 15 TO 20.

1 whole pork loin	2 teaspoons granulated garlic
1 tablespoon salt	1½ teaspoons dry Italian seasoning
2 teaspoons black pepper	Rhubarb Chutney (recipe follows)

Preheat oven to 400°F. Cut pork loin in half, where it was folded in the package. Rinse both pieces and pat dry. Rub both halves all over with the seasonings. Place in a roasting pan, fat side up. Place the pan in the center of the preheated oven and roast for approximately 30 minutes, until a meat thermometer registers 150° F for medium-roasted meat. Let the roast sit for 30 minutes, before slicing as thinly as possible. Serve warm with Scallion Biscuits (see page 91) and Rhubarb Chutney.

Rhubarb Chutney

Rhubarb is generally thought of as a New England thing, where it grows in many backyards, but many old-time Southerners are fond of it, as well. Fans of rhubarb love the tartness of the bright pink stalk, and think of it as a harbinger of spring.

MAKES ABOUT 1 QUART.

2 pounds fresh rhubarb, diced
1 large red onion, diced
1 box golden raisins
1½ pounds brown sugar
2 cups apple cider vinegar
2 tablespoons mustard seed

1 tablespoon whole
    cloves, tied in
    cheese cloth
2 teaspoons red pepper flakes
1½ tablespoons salt

Place everything in a heavy sauce pan and stir well. Bring to a boil, stirring occasionally, turn to simmer and cook for 30 minutes.

Keeps covered and refrigerated for up to 1 month.

Roasted Boneless Leg of Lamb with Watercress Pesto

This is the centerpiece of a classic spring feast. It's perfect for a Seder or Easter dinner. Boneless legs of lamb are actually easier to find now than bone-in legs, and are certainly a lot easier to work with. Lamb with Watercress Pesto may not be as classic a dish as lamb with mint jelly in this part of the world, but I think you'll enjoy the change.

SERVES 6 TO 8.

1 boneless leg of lamb
2 tablespoons olive oil
2 teaspoons chopped fresh garlic
2 teaspoons salt

1 teaspoon black pepper
2 teaspoons fresh rosemary leaves
Watercress Pesto (recipe follows)

Preheat oven to 400°F.

Rinse the leg of lamb and pat dry. Open the leg and butterfly by making a deep incision almost through the leg, allowing you to lay the leg out flat. Cut away large pieces of fat or gristle.

Rub the leg all over with the olive oil and seasonings. Place the seasoned leg in a roasting pan, cut side down. Place the pan in the middle of the preheated oven and cook to desired doneness. I prefer lamb medium rare, registering 135°F with a meat thermometer.

Let the meat rest for 20 minutes before slicing. Serve with Roasted New Potatoes (see page 126) and Watercress Pesto.

Watercress Pesto

Watercress grows wild in the cool streams of middle Tennessee, showing up in the first warm days of spring. Its peppery flavor and bright greenness are as invigorating as the waters of the stream itself. We intensify the flavor with a bit of strong Dijon mustard—wonderful with the richness of the lamb.

MAKES ABOUT 2 1/2 CUPS.

1 bunch watercress, thickest stems
   removed
2 cloves garlic
1 tablespoon Dijon mustard
½ cup Parmesan cheese

1 teaspoon salt
½ teaspoon black
   pepper
¾ cup olive oil

appetizers

salads

soups

vegetables & sides

entrees

desserts & pastries

Place all of the ingredients except the olive oil in the bowl of a food processor fitted with a steel blade. Turn the motor on and pour the olive oil through the feed tube while the mixture purees and emulsifies. Keeps covered and refrigerated for up to 1 week. Serve warm or room temperature with roasted or grilled meats, stirred into soups, or tossed with pasta.

Buttermilk Battered French Toast

This most desirable of breakfast plates is served year round, but we change the fruit with which the toast is topped seasonally. I like it best with berries, starting in the spring and through the summer. We use sautéed apples in winter and fall and dress it up with a sweetened cranberry puree.

SERVES 6.

Vegetable oil for deep frying
4 whole eggs, beaten
2 cups buttermilk
⅓ cup heavy cream
⅓ cup brown sugar

¼ teaspoon cinnamon
½ teaspoon vanilla
Pinch nutmeg
12 slices sourdough bread, cut in
    half, diagonally

Fill deep fryer with fresh oil to appropriate level. Heat oil to 350°F.

In a large mixing bowl, mix together all of the remaining ingredients except the bread. Thoroughly soak the bread in the egg mixture. Remove, allowing excess liquid to drip back into bowl. Deep fry until golden brown and cooked through, about 5 minutes.

Drain the French toast on a rack or paper towels, then plate and top with syrup, whipped cream and fresh berries.

Scallion Biscuits

Spring

appetizers

salads

soups

vegetables & sides

entrees

desserts & pastries

This is our "house bread." We vary it sometimes with dill, and we make sweet potato biscuits in colder months. This is not a classic Southern biscuit—it's really more of a scone. You will find it stays moist and tender much longer than the biscuits you grew up with.

MAKES ABOUT 25 BISCUITS.

2 cups flour
1 tablespoon plus ¾ teaspoon baking
    powder
½ teaspoon salt
2½ teaspoons sugar
¼ pound (1 stick) cold butter, diced

3 eggs, beaten
⅓ cup cream
1 scallion, green and
    white parts, sliced thin

Preheat oven to 350°F. Prepare a baking sheet with parchment paper or nonstick spray.

Mix dry ingredients in a food processor. Add diced butter and pulse.

Move to mixing bowl and mix in eggs, cream, and scallion. Roll out 1/2-inch thick, cut into 2-inch rounds, and bake at 350°F for 10 minutes.

Spinach, Mushroom, and Feta Quiche

We pride ourselves on having made quiche almost cool again. Like most things, quiche is as good as what you put in it. Fresh baby spinach, fresh mushrooms, and tangy feta cheese bound by eggs and heavy cream. How do you think it's going to taste?

MAKES 2 QUICHES, 8 TO 12 SERVINGS.

1 recipe piecrust (recipe follows)
2 tablespoons plus 2 tablespoons
   olive oil
1 onion, halved, then sliced thinly
¾ teaspoon plus ¼ teaspoon salt
½ teaspoon plus ¼ teaspoon
   black pepper
½ teaspoon dry Italian seasoning

2 quarts mushrooms, sliced
10 ounces feta cheese, crumbled
10 cups loosely packed baby
   spinach
14 eggs
2 cups cream

Preheat oven 375°F. Spray 2 deep 8-inch pie tins with nonstick spray. Roll out pie dough to 1/8 inch. Roll 1 circle of pie dough onto rolling pin and place over pie tin. Repeat with remaining dough. Fit pastries into tins and crimp edges. Place parchment paper over pastries and weight with dry beans or rice. Place tins in the center of the preheated oven and bake for 12 to 15 minutes, until the edges are beginning to brown. Remove parchment and weights, return to oven, and bake 5 minutes more. Remove from oven and set aside.

Prepare the filling. Heat 2 tablespoons olive oil in a sauté pan. Add onion and sauté with 3/4 teaspoon salt, 1/2 teaspoon pepper, and Italian seasoning for 5 minutes. Add mushrooms and cook for 3 more minutes. Remove from heat and set aside.

Heat remaining olive oil in a separate sauté pan. Add the spinach and toss to wilt the spinach, about 1 minute. Remove from heat.

In the prebaked pie shells, layer onion and mushrooms, feta, spinach, feta.

Beat together eggs and cream with remaining salt and pepper. Pour over filling. Place in the center of the preheated oven and bake for 35 to 40 minutes.

Piecrust

Spring

2 PIECRUSTS

3 cups all-purpose flour
2 teaspoons salt
4 tablespoons cold butter, cut
    into bits

4 tablespoons shortening
8 to 12 tablespoons ice water

Place the flour and salt in the bowl of a food processor fitted
with a stainless steel blade, and pulse to combine. Add the
butter and pulse until the butter is the size of tiny gravel. Add the shortening and
pulse to combine. Turn the motor on and add the ice water in bits until you have
a shaggy dough that will just hold together.

Gather the dough together and divide into 2 balls. Wrap each in plastic wrap
and refrigerate for 5 minutes before rolling out into 2 crusts and proceeding with
recipe.

Spring

appetizers

salads

soups

vegetables & sides

entrees

desserts & pastries

Lemon Muffins

I adore these muffins. We serve large ones for breakfast and baby ones for a ladies' lunch.

MAKES 8 MEDIUM OR 30 MINI-MUFFINS.

1¾ cups all-purpose flour

1 teaspoon baking powder

¾ teaspoon salt

¾ cup sugar

1 egg

6 tablespoons butter, melted

6 ounces sour cream

Zest and juice of 2 lemons

Preheat oven to 350°F. Line 8 (3-inch) muffin molds or 30 (1 1/2-inch) molds with baking cups.

Sift together the flour, baking powder, and salt.

In a large bowl, beat the sugar with the egg and melted butter. Add the dry ingredients to the egg mixture, along with the sour cream, and lemon juice and zest. Mix together well and pour into prepared muffin tins. Place in the center of the preheated oven and bake for approximately 10 minutes for small muffins, and 15 to 20 for larger, until cooked through and lightly browned.

Let cool slightly before removing from pans.

Strawberry Bread Pudding

appetizers

salads

soups

vegetables & sides

entrees

desserts & pastries

I don't know at what point in my life I decided that any food could be made into a bread pudding, but I haven't looked back since. This is very rich, very good, and very pink.

SERVES ABOUT 12.

(for the bread)
1 quart frozen strawberries, thawed
1 cup plus 1 cup sugar
4 eggs
3 cups all-purpose flour
1 teaspoon salt

1 teaspoon baking soda
1 teaspoon ground cinnamon
1¼ cups vegetable oil

Preheat oven to 350°F. Grease and flour 2 loaf pans.

   Place the strawberries and 1 cup sugar in the bowl of a food processor fitted with a steel blade. Pulse to mash the strawberries.

   In a mixing bowl, beat the eggs with the remaining cup of sugar. Set aside. In a large mixing bowl, sift the dry ingredients. Mix in the egg mixture, then the strawberries, then the oil. Pour into the prepared loaf pans. Place in the center of the preheated oven and bake for 1 hour. Let cool completely before turning out.

(for the bread pudding)
2 loaves strawberry bread
⅔ cup heavy cream

1 tablespoon sugar
1 teaspoon vanilla
2 eggs

Preheat oven to 325°F. Spray 1 baking sheet and 1 (9 x 5-inch or comparable) baking dish with nonstick spray.

   When the bread has cooled, cut it into 1-inch cubes. Turn these out onto the baking sheet and bake for 10 minutes to dry out a bit. Remove from oven and set aside.

   In a large mixing bowl, beat together the remaining ingredients. Add the cubed bread and toss. Pour into the prepared baking dish and bake for 30 to 40 minutes, until set and lightly browned. Serve with vanilla ice cream or whipped cream and fresh strawberries.

Spring

Pink Lemonade Mousse

This is the simplest thing in the world, and every little girl's favorite dish—especially our Moriah. Now there's a girly kind of girl. We serve it with berries and crispy cookies. What more could a girly-girl want?

SERVES 6.

1 envelope unflavored gelatin
¼ cup cold water
¾ cup frozen pink lemonade
      concentrate (or regular frozen
      lemonade concentrate with 1
      drop red food coloring),
      thawed

½ cup sugar
2 cups heavy cream, whipped

Sprinkle the gelatin over the water and allow to soften. Add the concentrate and sugar and stir to mix well. Simmer until the sugar and gelatin dissolve. Allow the mixture to cool and thicken slightly.

Temper a couple of spoons of cooled mousse into the whipped cream, then stir the cream back into the mousse. Spoon into parfait cups and chill. Serve topped with whipped cream and fresh berries with a sugar cookie on the side.

Lemon Layer Cake with Berry Filling and White Icing

appetizers

salads

soups

vegetables & sides

entrees

desserts & pastries

I believe we are the unofficial baby shower capitol of the world, and, as such, this cake, created by the fabulous Katherine, is our official mascot. Beautiful presented whole, breathtaking when it's sliced, and delicious through every bite.

SERVES ABOUT 12.

(for the cake)
1 cup butter, softened
2 cups sugar
Zest and juice of 1 lemon
3½ cups cake flour

3 teaspoons baking
    powder
¾ teaspoon salt
1 cup milk
8 egg whites

Preheat oven to 350°F. Line 4 (9-inch) cake pans with parchment, then spray with nonstick spray.

Cream the butter in an electric mixer. Add the sugar and beat until light. Add the lemon juice and zest.

Sift together the dry ingredients and add to the batter alternately with the milk, mixing well after each addition.

In a separate bowl, beat the egg whites until stiff but not dry. Fold the egg whites into the batter.

Evenly distribute the batter between the 4 pans, and bake in the preheated oven for about 25 minutes or until cakes test done. Remove from the oven and let cool in the pans before turning out onto cake racks. Let cool completely before assembling.

(for the filling)
2 cups Lemon Curd (recipe follows)

4 cups mixed berries (or berry of choice):
    whole raspberries and blueberries,
    chopped strawberries

Trim the cakes. Place one layer on a cake round and spread with a thin layer of lemon curd. Top with berries. Continue with next 2 layers. Top with final layer and spread entire cake with white icing.

Spring

appetizers

salads

soups

vegetables & sides

entrees

desserts & pastries

(for the icing)
1 stick butter

6 cups confectioners' sugar
3 tablespoons cream

Cream the butter with the sugar. Add the cream, a bit at a time, to reach spreading consistency.

Lemon Curd

MAKES ABOUT 1 2/3 CUPS.

2 cups sugar
3 eggs
Zest of 2 lemons

½ cup fresh squeezed lemon juice
6 tablespoons butter, cut in bits.

In a stainless steel sauce pan, whisk together the sugar, the eggs, and the lemon zest. Add the juice and the butter and cook, whisking, until the butter is melted. Continue to cook, whisking constantly, until the mixture is thickened.

Use a rubber spatula to scrape the curd through a sieve into a bowl. Let cool, cover the surface with plastic wrap, and refrigerate for 1 hour (or up to 1 week) to allow it to fully thicken.

Summer

As a child, summer was my favorite season. Besides having my two favorite events of the year—my birthday and the Fourth of July, summer was when the girls, my older sisters and Mama, a school teacher, were all together. More specifically, summer was when we were all together at Seven Hills swim club.

Nothing fancy, mind you. Just the right combination of lawn, concrete, and water. Summer held sounds of my older sister's Swinger radio tuned into WMAK. That in turn held the mysterious sadness of Otis Redding's "Sittin' on the Dock of the Bay," a sadness which angered me, but still, at age eight left me somehow more knowing, feeling somehow more like them—my sisters, that is.

So many coming of age stories are set in the summer. Is it the brightness of images and memory—the contrasts, the long days and longer nights? When I think of those days my senses are fairly bombarded. The broken Prell shampoo bottle lying in the concrete shower. Remember the vivid green of the shampoo, and the bright red blood? The mingling scents of Coppertone, cheeseburgers, and chlorine. The thrill of an all out dunking and splashing fight, until it stopped being fun.

But mainly, summer was fun, and bright, and loud. Just like summer food. Summer was the one time when our produce was truly local. What a difference it made in our tomatoes and corn, butterbeans, and okra. Summer was when I learned to love the vivid taste of vegetables and fruits. The joys of peaches and watermelon were strictly summertime joys, and you knew that you should appreciate them while you could: that these fruits, like the swimming club and the daylong company of the girls, would not be around forever.

I think that is the essence of summer: you need to suck the flavor out of every single day, every thunderstorm and ice cream cone, convertible ride, BLT, and lightning bug catch. The flavor is heady and the days won't last.

Mini BLT's

Summer

*We used to make open-faced tomato sandwiches on soft white
bread. They were delicious, but got sopping wet after an hour or
so. These BLT's on toast hold up much better, and pack a lot of
taste into 1 or 2 bites. Hands down our customers' favorite
summer hors d'oeuvre.*

appetizers

salads

soups

vegetables & sides

entrees

desserts & pastries

MAKES 36 PIECES.

12 slices sourdough bread
12 vine ripe Roma tomatoes
1 cup Homemade Mayonnaise
　　(see page 52)

1 cup Basil Pesto
　　(recipe follows)
4 slices cooked bacon, chopped fine

Preheat oven to 350°F. Use a 1 1/2-inch biscuit cutter to cut rounds out of the
bread. You should get at least 3 rounds per slice, depending on the size of the loaf.
Place the rounds on an ungreased baking sheet and toast until crispy throughout.

Slice tomatoes into 1/4-inch rounds.

Spread each toast round with Homemade Mayo, and top with a tomato slice.
Dollop a bit of Basil Pesto over the tomato and top with a sprinkle of bacon.

Basil Pesto

Basil costs like sin three-fourths of the year, but in the summer we have enough to swim in, so we make lots of Basil Pesto, and just swim in that instead.

Our pesto has no nuts—good for those with food allergies, easier on the pocket book, and it won't turn bitter, as some pesto with nuts are wont to do.

MAKES 3 CUPS.

2 cups basil leaves	½ teaspoon salt
2 cups Parmesan cheese	½ teaspoon black pepper
2 teaspoons chopped garlic	2 cups olive oil

Place all of the ingredients except the olive oil in the bowl of a food processor fitted with a steel blade. Start the food processor and slowly pour the olive oil through the feed tube. Process until smooth. Taste and adjust seasoning.

Corn Puddings with Cilantro and Parmesan

appetizers

salads

soups

vegetables & sides

entrees

desserts & pastries

I have this annoying habit of making up hors d'oeuvres—things that sound simply divine—and getting so excited that I sell them to large parties without quite thinking through the logistics of the enterprise. This was the case for a little party of 375 to whom I promised corn fritters. As the date of the party loomed nearer, I began to seriously consider frying 750 corn fritters. It was then that I created these savory bread puddings, which you bake all at once, then cut out with a biscuit cutter. Much more sensible for a crowd and truly, truly delicious. Happy guests, happy kitchen. What a wonderful world.

MAKES 3 DOZEN (2-INCH) SQUARES.

5 slices sourdough bread, cubed
1 tablespoon olive oil
½ red onion, sliced thinly
3 ears fresh corn
1 cup shredded Parmesan cheese
5 eggs

1 cup cream
1 teaspoon salt
¼ teaspoon cayenne
1 teaspoon ground cumin
1 bunch cilantro, roughly chopped

Preheat oven to 325°F. Spray a 9 x 11-inch or comparable jelly roll pan with non-stick spray. Place cubed bread in a large mixing bowl and set aside.

Heat the olive oil in a medium sauté pan and cook the onion over medium-high heat for 4 minutes. Add to mixing bowl with bread.

Cut the kernels from the corn and add to the bowl, along with the cheese.

Beat the eggs and cream with the seasonings. Pour into the bowl and mix well. Add the chopped cilantro and mix again.

Pour onto the prepared jelly roll pan, spreading evenly in an approximately 1 1/2-inch layer. Place in the center of the preheated oven and bake for 20 minutes, until puffed and set. Let cool before slicing into squares or cutting out circles with a small biscuit cutter. Serve warm or room temperature.

Fried Okra

Okra is the final test of the true Southern food hound. If you don't get it, you're not in the club. Even border-line hounds will gobble these up. Crispy, sweet, and tender.

SERVES 6.

1 pound very small okra, trimmed
1 cup buttermilk
2 cups self-rising flour
2 cups cornmeal

1 teaspoon salt
¼ teaspoon cayenne
¼ teaspoon black pepper
Oil for frying

In a mixing bowl, soak the okra in the buttermilk for 30 minutes or overnight.

In another mixing bowl, stir together the flour and cornmeal with the salt, cayenne, and pepper.

Dredge the okra in the flour mixture and place in a single layer on a cookie sheet. Refrigerate for at least 30 minutes or up to 2 hours.

Heat the oil in a deep fryer to 325°F. Fry the okra in small batches for 5 minutes, until crispy and brown. Drain well and serve hot with horseradish sauce.

Baked Vidalia Onion Dip

*Make this decadent, gooey, creamy, savory and slightly sweet
spread in early summer, when the Vidalias still abound. I got the
idea from my sister Mary who made something similar at the
lake for the Fourth of July. A perfect starter for hungry folks who
have been in (or by) the pool all day.*

MAKES ABOUT 2 QUARTS.

¼ pound (1 stick) butter

4 Vidalias sliced thin

2 eggs, lightly beaten

1 cup heavy cream

2 pieces sourdough bread, torn into small
    pieces or processed in the food
    processor

1 cup soft goat cheese

5 whole or slightly torn basil leaves

½ teaspoon salt

¼ teaspoon white pepper

4 tablespoons shredded Parmesan cheese

Preheat oven to 350°F. Spray a 2-quart casserole dish with nonstick spray.

Melt the butter in a large sauté pan and cook the Vidalias until very soft.

Place the onions in a large bowl and mix with remaining ingredients with
the exception of the Parmesan cheese. Pour the mixture into the prepared casserole and top with the Parmesan.

Place the casserole in the center of the preheated oven and bake for approximately 20 to 25 minutes, until the spread is puffed, set and slightly browned.

Serve warm with crackers.

Martha's Summer Roll

This is my version of the summer roll at my favorite Vietnamese restaurant. I don't know how authentic it is, but Martha's Summer Roll is the essence of a cool and refreshing appetizer. Wonderful to serve under the fan on the porch on a hot summer's night.

MAKES 6 SUMMER ROLLS.

6 large cooked shrimp, peeled, deveined, tails off

1 (4-ounce) package cellophane noodles

1 tablespoon soy sauce

1 teaspoon brown sugar

Juice of 1 lime

1 package rice paper wrappers

1 cucumber, peeled, seeded and cut into thin strips

1 carrot, peeled and grated

1 bunch fresh basil

1 bunch fresh mint

1 tablespoon toasted sesame seeds

Asian Dipping Sauce (recipe follows)

Slice the shrimp in half, then set aside.

Soak the cellophane noodles in hot water for 5 minutes, or until soft. Drain and place in a bowl. Toss the noodles with the soy sauce, brown sugar, and lime juice. Soak 1 rice paper wrapper in warm water until pliable, about 1 minute. Place on a clean dish towel, then on a cutting board. Place 2 shrimp halves on the lower third of the wrapper, then a bit of the noodles, topped with 3 strips of cucumber, 1 tablespoon grated carrot, one or two basil leaves, and a few mint leaves, then sprinkle with sesame seeds. Fold the sides of the wrapper in, then roll up like a spring roll. Be careful not to roll too tightly, or they will tear. Don't get frustrated! It takes some trying to get the hang of it. If you are not serving the rolls immediately, wrap individually in cellophane and refrigerate for up to 3 hours. Serve with Asian Dipping Sauce.

Asian Dipping Sauce

I use this generic Asian-style sauce for everything from egg rolls and wontons to grilled tuna or pork. Clean and simple tastes are so good in the summer.

MAKES ABOUT 2 CUPS.

⅓ cup soy sauce
⅓ cup water
⅓ cup seasoned rice wine vinegar
1 tablespoon fish sauce
1 tablespoon brown sugar
Juice of two limes
1 tablespoon sambal oelek (Asian chili sauce)

1 tablespoon grated carrot
1 tablespoon grated daikon or radish
1 tablespoon sliced scallions
1 tablespoon grated ginger
1 teaspoon toasted sesame seeds

Mix together well.

Fresh Corn Cakes with Black-Eyed Pea Salsa

This is a party-sized take-off on something I grew up eating for breakfast on lazy summer weekends. They're a delicious little pop in the mouth. The cornmeal helps keep them stable enough to reheat for parties.

MAKES ABOUT 4 DOZEN 2 1/2-INCH CORN CAKES.

1¼ cups yellow cornmeal
¾ cup all-purpose flour
1¾ teaspoons baking powder
1 tablespoon sugar
¾ teaspoons salt
¼ teaspoon black pepper
Pinch cayenne
1⅔ cups buttermilk
4 tablespoons butter, melted

2 large eggs
2 ears white corn, kernels
   removed and cobs discarded
3 scallions, greens and white
   parts, thinly sliced
1 cup sour cream
Black-Eyed Pea Salsa (recipe
   follows)

Lightly grease and heat a griddle or flat sauté pan to medium heat.

In a large bowl, whisk together the dry ingredients.

In another large bowl, whisk together the buttermilk, melted butter, and eggs.

Make a well in the dry ingredients and pour the wet mixture into this. Mix together lightly until just combined.

Stir in the corn kernels and the scallions.

Spoon 1 tablespoon batter onto the griddle for each pancake. Cook until bubbles form on the surface, then turn and cook until underside is lightly browned.

Serve warm with sour cream (1/4 teaspoon per cake) and the Black-Eyed Pea Salsa. They may be cooled and reheated in a 350°F oven for 5 to 10 minutes.

Black-Eyed Pea Salsa

As wonderful as this is in the summer, made with fresh (and expensive) black-eyed peas, we make this salsa year round using frozen ones, and have gotten no complaints. We serve Black-Eyed Pea Salsa with Fresh Corn Cakes, Crawfish Cakes (see page 5), and as a dip with chips.

MAKES ABOUT 2 QUARTS.

appetizers

salads

soups

vegetables & sides

entrees

desserts & pastries

2 cups fresh black-eyed peas (frozen may be used if fresh are unavailable)
2 teaspoons salt
½ red onion, finely diced
1 (14½-ounce) can roasted red pepper, drained and chopped
3 large fresh tomatoes, diced

3 tablespoons rice wine vinegar
½ teaspoon cumin
2 teaspoons fresh chopped garlic
1 tablespoon chopped fresh mint
1 tablespoon chopped fresh cilantro

If using fresh black-eyed peas, rinse and sort them in a colander under cold water. Place in a medium sauce pan, cover with water by double their volume, add the salt, and bring to a boil on top of the stove. Skim off the scum, turn the heat to a slow boil and cook approximately 15 minutes, until the peas are quite tender, but not falling apart. Drain and let cool.

If using frozen peas, they may be added directly to the water, and cooked in the same manner as the fresh peas. Frozen peas will need to cook a bit longer than fresh, approximately 25 minutes. Drain and cool when tender.

In a large bowl, mix the peas with the remaining ingredients. Taste and adjust seasoning.

Snap Beans Tossed with Tomatoes and Roasted Corn

This is my favorite green vegetable of summer. When the beans are really fresh, they don't need to be long-cooked, the old "Southern" way. These blanched and marinated vegetables, served room temperature, are wonderful for entertaining, and add a nice jolt of color to the plate.

SERVES 6 TO 8.

2 ears corn, kernels cut from the cob	2 ripe tomatoes, rinsed and diced
2 teaspoons plus 2 tablespoons olive oil	½ red onion, sliced in thin half-circles
Pinch salt and pepper	1 tablespoon white wine vinegar
½ pound fresh snap beans, stem-end removed, and strung if necessary	1 bunch fresh cilantro, roughly chopped
	1 teaspoon ground cumin
	Salt and pepper to taste

Preheat oven to 400°F. On a baking sheet, toss the corn kernels with the 2 teaspoons olive oil and a pinch of salt and pepper. Roast in the oven for 15 minutes. Let cool and toss in a mixing bowl.

While the corn is roasting, bring a pot of salted water to a boil. Add the beans and cook until just tender (about 3 minutes if the beans are really good and fresh). Drain and cool completely in a bowl of ice water. Remove from the ice water, pat dry, and place in the same bowl as the corn.

Add the remaining ingredients and gently toss. Adjust seasoning and serve cool or room temperature.

Seared Salmon Salad

Summer

*This makes a fabulous luncheon dish, on a little bed of lettuce
topped with grape tomatoes and basil. We sell the heck out of it at
the restaurant. It's so good for you, and delicious, too.*

SERVES 6 TO 8.

2 tablespoons olive oil
2½ pounds fresh salmon, skinned and
    filleted and cut into 5 to 6 ounce
    portions
1 teaspoon salt
½ teaspoon black pepper
½ small red onion, very thinly sliced
Inner ribs and leaves of 1 bunch celery,
    very thinly sliced

Juice and zest of 4
    lemons
3 tablespoons capers
4 tablespoon flat leaf
    parsley, rough chopped
4 tablespoons olive oil
1 teaspoon red pepper flakes
Salt (if needed)

Heat the olive oil in a large nonstick skillet. Season the salmon with salt and
pepper, and sear in the olive oil, cut side down over medium-high heat, approximately 4 minutes on the first side, then 3 minutes on the skin side. If the salmon
has not reached desired doneness, place in a preheated 400°F oven for 2 or 3
minutes. Remove the salmon from the skillet, place on a rack and let cool.

Break salmon into chunks and place in a large mixing bowl. Add the
remaining ingredients and toss lightly to combine.

Serve cool on bed of greens with Grape Tomato and Basil Salad (recipe
follows).

Grape Tomato and Basil Salad

Tomatoes are always best left unrefrigerated, so prepare this salad close to serving time. If you must refrigerate the salad, be sure to let it come to room temperature before serving. This is also delicious tossed with hot pasta and topped with crumbled feta cheese.

SERVES 6.

2 pints grape or cherry tomatoes,
    cut in half
½ red onion, sliced thinly
    lengthwise
4 cloves garlic, minced
3 tablespoons olive oil

2 tablespoons red wine vinegar
1 teaspoon brown sugar
Salt and black pepper to taste
¼ cup packed fresh basil leaves,
    roughly chopped

Mix everything together and let rest for 30 minutes to let the flavors marry.

Roasted Summer Vegetables

These roasted vegetables are as intensely sunny as the day itself. A wonderful accompaniment for simple grilled meats, or a light luncheon item on its own.

appetizers

salads

soups

vegetables & sides

entrees

desserts & pastries

SERVES 8 TO 10.

2 yellow squash, cut into ¼-inch circles
2 zucchini, cut into ¼-inch circles
2 tablespoons plus 3 tablespoons olive oil
1 teaspoon plus 1 teaspoon salt
¼ teaspoon plus ¼ teaspoon black pepper
1 eggplant, quartered lengthwise, then cut into ¼-inch slices
1 red onion, thinly sliced
1 can roasted red peppers, drained and roughly chopped

2 teaspoons fresh garlic, roughly chopped
1 tablespoon honey
3 tablespoons red wine vinegar
1 tablespoon roughly chopped flat leaf parsley

Preheat the oven to 400°F. Spray 2 baking sheets with nonstick spray.

Toss the sliced yellow squash and zucchini together on a sheet pan with 2 tablespoons olive oil, 1 teaspoon salt, and 1/4 teaspoon black pepper. Spread them out quite thinly. Do not stack! Do the same on a separate pan with eggplant and onion. Roast the squash for approximately 15 minutes, and the eggplant and onion for 20, until nicely browned and softened. Remove and let cool for 5 minutes.

Toss the cooled roasted vegetables in a large mixing bowl with the remaining ingredients. Mix lightly, being careful not to break up the vegetables. Season to taste and serve warm or at room temperature.

Baby Limas with Basil

I can't tell you how many people have told me that they hated lima beans until they tried these. It's no great secret, I just treat them with a little respect, cook them just right, and give them the seasoning they deserve. Isn't that what we all want?

SERVES 6.

1 pound fresh or frozen baby
  limas
2 teaspoons salt
1 tablespoon fresh garlic,
  chopped
½ cup olive oil

1 red onion, thinly sliced
¼ cup tarragon vinegar
¼ cup fresh basil, roughly
  chopped (or mint in spring)
½ teaspoon black pepper

If using fresh limas, rinse and sort in a colander under cold water. Place in a medium sauce pan, cover with salted water by double their volume, and bring to a boil. Skim off the scum, turn down to a slow boil and cook until tender (better too tender than not tender enough), about 15 minutes. Frozen limas may be placed directly in the water, and will probably need 20 to 25 minutes to cook.

Drain the tender limas, place in a mixing bowl, and toss with the garlic and olive oil while still warm. Let cool, then stir in the onion, vinegar, basil, and pepper. Taste for seasoning and serve room temperature.

Summer Harvest Salad with Fresh Field Peas and Tomato

This salad tastes like the Fourth of July—crisp and bold and juicy. The really good tomatoes are finally here, and it's time to show them off. This is just the ticket.

SERVES 6 TO 8.

1 cup fresh field peas (crowders, black eyes, creamers, or pink eyes)
2 teaspoons salt
2 ears fresh corn
3 green onions, sliced thinly
2 tomatoes, diced
1 cup Lemon-Thyme Vinaigrette (see page 85)

2 hearts of Romaine lettuce, cut into bite-size pieces
2 cups croutons
½ cup feta cheese, crumbled

Rinse and sort the peas in a colander under cold water. Place in a medium sauce pan, cover with salted water by double their volume, and bring to a boil. Skim the scum, turn down to a slow boil, and cook until tender, approximately 15 minutes. Drain and rinse under cool water. Place in a mixing bowl and set aside.

While the peas are cooking, bring another pot of salted water to a boil. Add the corn and cook for 5 minutes. Drain and cool. Cut the kernels from the corn and add to the mixing bowl, along with the green onions and tomatoes. Toss with the Lemon-Thyme Vinaigrette.

Place the hearts of Romaine in a serving bowl, top with the field pea mixture, the croutons, and feta cheese. Serve immediately.

❈

Summer

appetizers

salads

soups

vegetables & sides

entrees

desserts & pastries

New Potato Salad Vinaigrette

Potato salad is like a pair of khaki pants. Good ones can take you anywhere you want to go, especially in the summer to match with things like fried chicken and burgers.

It took me years to get potato salad right, and when I finally figured it out, I felt as if I had been quite silly for so long. The simple trick is in the draining. Once you drain your potatoes, you must resist the temptation to rinse them or stop their cooking by running them under cold water. Rinsing a potato washes away all of their starch, the stuff that binds a potato salad—makes it cling together. So no rinsing! This little secret could change your life.

SERVES 6 TO 8.

1½ quarts small red skin potatoes, cut in
   half
1 tablespoon plus 1 teaspoon salt
¼ small red onion, finely diced
2 ribs celery, finely diced
1 tablespoon flat leaf parsley, coarsely
   chopped

2 teaspoons Dijon mustard
2 teaspoons white wine vinegar
3 tablespoons olive oil
¼ teaspoon black pepper

Place the potatoes in a medium pot and cover with water. Add the tablespoon salt and bring to a boil. Cook until just tender, approximately 15 minutes. Drain the potatoes and do not rinse. Let them cool about 5 minutes (they should still be warm), then place the potatoes in a large mixing bowl.

Stir in the remaining ingredients and adjust the seasoning to taste. This is fabulous served barely warm. If you must refrigerate the salad before serving, let it come back to room temperature.

Greek Orzo Salad

Let me say this: I am not a pasta salad fan. Generally speaking, I think a noodle wants eating right after it has been cooked. The texture changes so dramatically when it has been sitting for awhile, and not, to my mind, for the better. That being said, I really love this salad made with orzo pasta. I think the tiny shape of the pasta keeps it from getting too starchy, and the flavors are all of my favorite briny, Mediterranean-inspired things: capers, peppers, feta, and lemon. Wonderful tastes for a sun-kissed day.

SERVES 6 TO 8.

2 cups orzo pasta
4 tablespoons olive oil
½ cup crumbled feta cheese
2 ribs celery, diced
¼ red onion, sliced radially
Juice and zest of 1 lemon
1 garlic clove, minced
2 tablespoons flat leaf parsley, roughly chopped
¼ cup pitted Kalamata olives, sliced in half, lengthwise

2 scallions, greens and white parts, sliced thinly
¼ cup pepperoncini peppers, stemmed and sliced thinly
2 tablespoons capers
1 tablespoon tarragon vinegar
Salt to taste
¼ teaspoon red pepper flakes (or to taste)

Cook the pasta in plenty of well-salted, boiling water until just cooked through, approximately 5 minutes. Drain the pasta in a colander, and cool under running cold water.

Place the pasta in a large mixing bowl and add the olive oil, tossing to coat well. Add the remaining ingredients and mix well.

Chilled Squash Soup with Coriander and Mint

Coriander is rubbed, dried cilantro, but the taste is quite different, subtle and slightly smoky. It takes an old Southern favorite and makes it a bit more hip.

SERVES 6.

1 teaspoon vegetable oil	Pinch cayenne
½ medium white onion, diced	6 medium yellow squash
2 cups chicken stock	1 cup buttermilk
1 teaspoon salt	1 cup heavy cream
½ teaspoon coriander	1 tablespoon fresh mint
¼ teaspoon black pepper	1 cup diced fresh tomato

Heat the oil in a 2 to 3-quart sauce pan and sauté the onion about 5 minutes. Pour in the stock and seasonings and bring to a boil. Add the squash and cook about 15 minutes.

Let cool, then roughly puree. Place in a bowl and stir in the buttermilk, cream, and mint. Taste for seasoning and serve cold. Garnish with diced tomatoes.

Martha's Gazpacho

Summer

Our Gazpacho is a hybrid from many, many that I have tasted through the years. I don't even pretend to call it authentic, but who cares? It tastes terrific.

SERVES 10 TO 12.

4 cucumbers, seeded and diced
1 (32-ounce) can diced tomatoes
½ cup flat leaf parsley, roughly chopped
½ cup cilantro, roughly chopped
½ cup fresh basil, roughly chopped
1 small red onion, small dice
Juice of 3 lemons
1 (14-ounce) can roasted red pepper, drained and diced or processed

2 tablespoons Louisiana-style hot sauce
2 tablespoons olive oil
1 cup water
2 teaspoons minced fresh garlic
2 (14-ounce) cans tomato juice
2 tablespoons white wine vinegar

Combine all ingredients and taste for seasoning.

appetizers

salads

soups

vegetables & sides

entrees

desserts & pastries

Roasted Tomato Soup

This soup is a case study in simple, bold flavor. Wonderfully ripe tomatoes, intensified by roasting, enhanced with thyme and red wine. Perfect!

SERVES 6 TO 8.

2 pounds ripe tomatoes	3 sprigs fresh thyme
2 tablespoons olive oil	1 cup red wine
½ teaspoon salt	2 cups chicken stock
½ teaspoon black pepper	

Preheat the oven to 400°F.

Place the tomatoes in a roasting pan. Add the olive oil, salt, pepper, and fresh thyme and toss with the tomatoes to coat well. Place in the center of the preheated oven and roast for 30 to 40 minutes, until the tomato skins crack and begin to brown. Remove from the oven and let cool.

When cool enough to handle, remove the skins and discard. Pull the thyme leaves from the stems and discard the stems. Working in batches, place the roasted tomatoes along with their juices and the thyme leaves, in the bowl of a food processor fitted with a stainless steel blade. Roughly puree the tomatoes and place in a soup pot. Add the wine and chicken stock and bring to a boil. Turn to low and cook for 20 minutes. Taste and adjust the seasoning and serve warm with Sourdough Croutons (see page 65).

Chilled Honeydew Soup

This unique and refreshing soup may become a summertime addiction. There are worse habits to have.

SERVES 6 TO 8.

1 large honeydew, cubed
1 teaspoon green curry paste
1 can unsweetened coconut milk
2 tablespoons fresh mint, roughly chopped
Juice of 1 lime
4 tablespoons shredded coconut, toasted

Place the cubed melon in the bowl of a food processor fitted with a stainless steel blade. Add the remaining ingredients, except the coconut, and process until smooth. Taste and adjust the seasoning. Serve chilled, garnished with the toasted coconut.

Summer Succotash

I am enchanted by fresh field peas. Those truly seasonal summer-time treats that finally appear in late June, in the leftover tops of cardboard boxes, next to the register at the farmers' market. I want to run my hands through them, like a kid in a sand box or a pirate with a chest full of gold. Pity the poor shopper behind me who watches in disbelief as I empty every single pea from every box top. Crowders, creamers, purple eyes, limas, black eyes, and finally October beans—I cannot pass them by. The season is too short and each pea too precious to me.

You treat fresh field peas delicately—they don't need much to accent their God-given flavor. This Summer Succotash uses a light hand, with the freshest vegetables and a shorter cooking time. Enjoy it while you can.

SERVES 6 TO 8.

½ pound fresh baby lima beans
½ pound fresh crowder peas
½ pound fresh black-eyed peas
2 tablespoons olive oil
1 small red onion, diced
2 ears silver queen corn, kernels removed
   and cobs discarded

½ pound small fresh okra pods, trimmed
   and sliced to ½-inch
3 large homegrown tomatoes, diced
4 cups chicken stock
Salt and pepper to taste
Juice of 1 to 2 limes
1 bunch cilantro, roughly chopped

Rinse and sort the limas in a colander under cold running water. Place in a medium sauce pan and cover by double their volume with salted water. Bring to a boil, skim off the scum, turn the heat to a slow boil and cook until tender, approximately 10 to 15 minutes. Do the same with the crowders and black eyes, cooking each in a separate pot. When tender, you may drain them together, rinse and set aside.

Heat the olive oil in a soup pot. Add the onion and cook for 4 minutes. Add the corn, okra, tomatoes, and all of the cooked field peas to the pot. Pour in the chicken stock and bring to a boil. Turn to a simmer and cook for 10 minutes. Season to taste with the salt and pepper and the lime juice. Stir in the cilantro and serve hot.

Chilled Cucumber Soup

Not your bland cooked cucumber kind of thing, this soup is crisp and refreshing. A perfect starter on a hot summer night.

SERVES 6 TO 8.

appetizers

salads

soups

vegetables & sides

entrees

desserts & pastries

6 medium cucumbers, peeled,
    seeded and roughly chopped
¼ red onion, roughly chopped
1½ cups cold chicken stock
1 teaspoon salt

¼ teaspoon white pepper
½ teaspoon turmeric
2 cups heavy cream
¼ cup roughly chopped mint
    leaves

Using a blender and working in 2 or 3 batches, puree the cucumbers with the red onion and chicken stock. Stir in the seasoning and the cream. Taste and adjust the seasoning. Serve chilled with the chopped mint.

Roasted New Potatoes

I love these with the grilled tastes of summer, particularly with flank steak, but also with chicken, pork, or even grilled fish. The mint is a bit unexpected, with a fresher taste than the rosemary you usually find.

SERVES 6 TO 8.

2 pounds new red skin potatoes	1 teaspoon salt
	½ teaspoon black pepper
3 tablespoons olive oil	1 tablespoon fresh mint, roughly chopped

Preheat oven to 400°F. Cut new potatoes into bite-sized cubes. On a baking sheet, toss with olive oil, salt, and pepper. Bake for 20 minutes, until nicely browned and cooked through. Remove from oven and let cool slightly.

Toss with mint and serve warm.

Squash Casserole

This is my latest update on the most popular dish I prepared on Martha Stewart Living. With all of the cheese and bread crumbs, I consider it more of a starch than a vegetable dish. Nothing can beat it straight out of the oven with a crispy brown crust, all bubbly, and cheesy underneath. This one dish could make you very popular.

appetizers

salads

soups

vegetables & sides

entrees

desserts & pastries

SERVES 8 TO 10.

2 pounds yellow squash, cut in ½-inch circles

1 Vidalia onion, coarsely chopped

1 tablespoon plus 1 teaspoon salt

3 eggs, beaten

1 cup cream

1 teaspoon fresh thyme (or ½ teaspoon dried)

½ teaspoon black pepper

1 cup plus ½ cup unseasoned dry bread crumbs

¾ cup plus ½ cup grated sharp white cheddar

Place the squash and onion in a large pot, cover with water, add the tablespoon salt and bring to a boil. Cook for 20 minutes and drain well.

Preheat the oven to 350°F. Spray a 9 x 11-inch baking dish with nonstick spray.

Whisk together the eggs and cream with the thyme, remaining salt, and black pepper.

Place drained vegetables in a large mixing bowl with bread crumbs, egg mixture, seasoning, and 3/4 cup cheese. Mix well and pour into prepared baking dish. Top with additional bread crumb and remaining cheese.

Cover the baking dish with aluminum foil and bake in the center of the pre-heated oven for 30 minutes. Remove the foil and bake 10 minutes more. Serve warm.

Tomato Eggplant Stew

Okay, it's ratatouille. But I own a Southern restaurant, and I'm not talking the South of France. If I can grow all of those vegetables in my own backyard, I figure I can call it what I like. And it sure tastes good. It tastes even better after 1 or 2 days.

SERVES 10 TO 12.

½ cup olive oil
1 onion, diced
2 yellow squash, cut into 1-inch
    cubes
2 zucchini, cut into 1-inch cubes
1 eggplant, partially peeled in
    wide strips, cut into 1-inch
    cubes

2 tablespoons garlic
1 can roasted red pepper, drained
    and roughly chopped
½ can tomato strips
1 cup red wine
2 teaspoons salt
½ teaspoon red pepper flakes
10 leaves fresh basil, roughly torn

Heat the olive oil in a deep-sided skillet, add the onion and cook 4 minutes. Add the yellow squash, zucchini, and eggplant and cook for 10 minutes. Add remaining ingredients, except fresh basil. Stir and cook for 30 minutes. Stir in basil. Taste and adjust seasoning.

No-Fail Fried Corn

*Fried corn for cheaters, or perfectionists, depending on your view.
I was taught growing up that adding flour was cheating, that you
didn't have to if you had some good, starchy field corn. These
days field corn's right hard to get ahold of, and the flour sure does
help. I won't tell if you won't.*

SERVES 8 TO 10.

8 slices bacon
12 ears white corn
3 tablespoons flour
2 cups milk
Salt and pepper to taste

In a heavy skillet, cook the bacon until crispy. Remove and reserve for another
use (a BLT is always a good idea).

Add the corn to the bacon fat and stir to coat. Cook for 10 minutes, allowing
some bits of corn to slightly brown before stirring. Add the flour and cook, stirring for 5 minutes. Stir in the milk and cook for 15 minutes. Adjust the consistency with more milk or flour. Season to taste with salt and pepper.

Summer

Roasted Crookneck Squash with Grape Tomatoes and Pesto

My complaint with summer squash is that the moisture content's so high, sometimes it just tastes like water. A quick blanch, a slow roast, and a toss in the pesto cure all of that, coaxing summer squash to its flavorful peak.

SERVES 6 TO 8.

2 teaspoons salt
1 pound small yellow crookneck
 squash, trimmed

2 tablespoons olive oil
1 pint grape tomatoes
½ cup Basil Pesto (see page 104)

Preheat the oven to 400°F.

Bring a large pot of water to a boil with the salt. Add the squash and cook until just tender, about 5 minutes. Drain well.

Place the squash in a mixing bowl with the olive oil and tomatoes, tossing to coat.

Spread the vegetables out on an ungreased baking sheet, place in the middle of the oven and roast for 20 minutes. Remove from the oven and let cool slightly. Toss with the pesto and serve warm.

Roasted Tomatoes Stuffed with Chèvre

Summer

appetizers

salads

soups

vegetables & sides

entrees

desserts & pastries

There's not much you need to say about this, but let it cool a bit so you don't burn yourself on the juiciness of it all. This is really, really good. Simple things usually are.

SERVES 8.

2 cups soft chèvre
1 egg, beaten
½ teaspoon fresh garlic, chopped
5 to 6 fresh basil leaves, chopped
¼ teaspoon red pepper flakes

8 firm, ripe tomatoes
½ cup dry bread
   crumbs

Preheat oven to 350°F. Spray a 9 x 11-inch or comparable baking dish with non-stick spray.

    Place the chèvre and egg in a mixing bowl with the garlic, basil, and pepper flakes. Use a fork to combine thoroughly.

    From the top of each tomato (not the stem end), cut out a cone-shaped piece, deep enough to hold 2 tablespoons of chèvre. Set the tomatoes in the baking dish on their stem end. Stuff the cavity with the goat cheese and sprinkle the top with bread crumbs.

    Place in the middle of the preheated oven and bake for 15 to 20 minutes, until the cheese is puffed and slightly browned, but the tomato not falling apart (exact time will depend on the ripeness of the tomato). Serve warm.

Stewed Okra

Okra for dummies. No slime, loads of garlic, tomato, and other good stuff. Even Yankees get this.

SERVES 6 TO 8.

3 tablespoons olive oil
1 red onion, chopped medium
2 teaspoons fresh garlic, chopped
1 pound small okra, trimmed and
    cut into ½-inch circles
4 fresh tomatoes, diced

1 tablespoon red wine vinegar
1 cup red wine
2 to 3 cups water
Salt and pepper to taste
3 tablespoons flat leaf parsley,
    roughly chopped

Heat the olive oil in a deep heavy skillet. Add the onion and cook 4 minutes. Add the garlic and okra and cook 5 minutes. Add the tomato, stir, and cook 5 minutes. Add the vinegar, the wine, and 2 cups water. Bring the mixture to a boil, turn to simmer, and cook until the okra is tender—20 to 30 minutes. Add more water as necessary to prevent the dish from drying out. Season to taste with salt and pepper, stir in the parsley, and serve warm.

Slow Roasted Pork Loin with Peach Barbecue Sauce

Like most modern restaurateurs, I heavily promote the consumption of medium-rare pork, and warn against the dangers of lean meat drying out. That said, this slow roast is sooooo good taken to a medium doneness. I leave the layer of fat on top of the loin as its natural moisturizer. As the roast cooks, the fat melts down and permeates the meat. Mmmmm. Pork is good.

SERVES 15 TO 20.

1 whole pork loin	1 teaspoon chili powder
1 tablespoon salt	2 teaspoons ground cumin
2 teaspoons black pepper	Peach Barbecue Sauce (recipe follows).
2 teaspoons granulated garlic	

Preheat oven to 400°F. Cut pork loin in half, where it was folded in the package. Rinse both pieces and pat dry. Rub both halves all over with the seasonings. Place in a roasting pan, fat side up. Place the pan in the center of the preheated oven and roast for approximately 30 minutes, until a meat thermometer registers 150°F for medium-roasted meat. Let the roast sit for 30 minutes, before slicing thinly. Pile over Corn Light Bread (see page 146) and serve open-faced with Peach Barbecue Sauce.

Peach Barbecue Sauce

If you're in a major hurry, take a good jar of barbecue sauce and some thawed frozen peaches. Chop up the peaches, add to the sauce and heat it up on top of the stove. Shh. Don't tell.

MAKES ABOUT 2 QUARTS.

2 tablespoons olive oil
½ red onion, diced
1 tablespoon chopped garlic
1 (28-ounce) can plum tomatoes, roughly chopped in food processor, with juice
¼ cup tomato ketchup
2 tablespoons Dijon mustard

3 tablespoons light brown sugar
1 tablespoon molasses
2 tablespoons soy sauce
2 tablespoons Louisiana-style hot sauce
1 quart cubed peaches (about 3 to 4 peaches)

Heat the olive oil in a sauce pan over medium heat. Add the onion and sauté for 4 minutes. Add the garlic, cook 1 minute, then add the remaining ingredients except the peaches. Bring to a boil, reduce heat to simmer, and cook for 30 minutes. Add the peaches and cook 10 minutes more. Taste and adjust seasoning.

Marinated Grilled Flank Steak with Roasted Summer Vegetables and Creamy Basil Chèvre

appetizers

salads

soups

vegetables & sides

entrees

desserts & pastries

We first served this for a very large dinner party, slightly formal, held out-of-doors at the end of the summer. The hostess asked for a lighter entree, but with red meat, and something that wouldn't have to be served piping hot. The flank steak was perfect! So flavorful with the marinade and the smoke from the grill, we served it like a great big salad over field greens with Roasted Summer Vegetables and Creamy Basil Chèvre dressing. Elegant and easy is usually the ticket for a hot summer night.

SERVES 6.

(for the marinade)
3 cloves garlic, minced
Juice and zest of 2 lemons
3 tablespoons olive oil

2 teaspoons fresh thyme leaves
  (or ½ teaspoon dried)
¼ teaspoon black pepper
Pinch cayenne

In a large mixing bowl, whisk together the garlic, lemon juice and zest, olive oil, and seasonings.

(for the entree)
2 pounds (about 2 flank steaks) rinsed and
  patted dry

Roasted Summer Vegetables (see page 115)
Creamy Basil Chèvre (recipe follows)

Thoroughly coat the flank steak with the marinade. Cover and refrigerate for at least 1 hour and up to 24.

Heat a grill to medium heat. Remove the flank steak from the bowl, and blot dry on paper towels. Place the flank steak on the hot grill and cook for approximately 5 minutes per side. Be sure to let the flank steak brown nicely on the first side before attempting to turn it. The crust that forms will actually lift the flesh away from the grill, making it much easier to turn.

Allow grilled flank to sit for 5 minutes before slicing as thinly as you can. Serve over field greens with Roasted Summer Vegetables and Creamy Basil Chèvre.

❊

135

Creamy Basil Chèvre

The basil really makes this sauce—turns it a tender shade of green, and gives a lingering aroma people can't quite place.

MAKES ABOUT 1 1/2 CUPS.

1 cup soft chèvre
2 teaspoon tarragon vinegar
½ teaspoon chopped fresh garlic
¼ teaspoon black pepper
4 to 5 basil leaves

Place all of the ingredients in the bowl of a food processor fitted with a steel blade. Blend thoroughly.

Taste for seasoning and serve room temperature. Store covered in the refrigerator for up to 1 week.

Fried Chicken

Of course we eat chicken throughout the year, but summer has to be the official fried chicken season. I remember stopping in south Alabama for a cold fried chicken picnic every June on the way to Ft. Walton, Florida. Gnawing on a fried chicken leg and looking up at all that Spanish moss, I knew I was this close to heaven.

Using boneless meat makes this chicken especially nice for picnics, luncheons, and even seated dinners. Buttermilk makes the chicken tender. Breading the chicken ahead of time makes for an extra crispy crust.

SERVES 6.

6 (6-ounce) boneless, skinless chicken breasts, rinsed and patted dry
2 cups buttermilk
3 cups self-rising flour
2 teaspoons salt
½ teaspoons black pepper
¼ teaspoons cayenne
¼ teaspoons garlic powder
Vegetable oil for frying

In a nonreactive bowl or other container, combine the chicken and the buttermilk. Turn the breasts to coat thoroughly, cover and refrigerate for at least an hour.

Line a baking sheet with wax or parchment paper. In another mixing bowl, combine the flour, salt, pepper, cayenne, and garlic powder. Remove the chicken breasts from the buttermilk one at a time and dredge in the flour mixture. Place the dredged breasts on the lined baking sheet. Cover and refrigerate for at least 30 minutes or up to 3 hours.

In a deep fryer, heat vegetable oil to 350°F. Cook the chicken in the hot oil for approximately 8 minutes, until nicely browned and cooked through. Drain the cooked chicken, then serve with Country Gravy (recipe follows). Chicken can be fried up to 2 hours ahead of time, then heated, uncovered, in a 375°F oven for 10 to 15 minutes. Chicken may also be served cold without the gravy.

Country Gravy

Country Gravy is what you put on your chicken if you're eating it on a plate. This is what you do on Sundays for supper, when you eat in the dining room. On these occasions you eat mashed potatoes instead of potato salad. Then you go lie down.

It's the milk that makes this a country-style gravy. City folks tend to just use stock.

SERVES 6.

3 tablespoons oil from frying chicken

3 tablespoons flour

4 cups milk, heated

Salt and pepper, to taste

Dash paprika

Heat the oil in a sauce pan on medium-high heat. Whisk in the flour. Cook, stirring constantly, for 3 minutes. Slowly whisk in half of the milk and bring to a simmer. As the gravy thickens, stir in additional milk until you reach the consistency you desire. (You may not use all of the milk.) Season to taste and serve over fried chicken, pork chops, or country fried steak.

Gravy may be made 1 day ahead of time, then covered and refrigerated until ready to use. Reheat slowly over medium-low heat.

Crispy Grouper with Smoked Tomato Vinaigrette

appetizers

salads

soups

vegetables & sides

entrees

desserts & pastries

Grouper is a magnificent fish, milky white and firm of flesh, that's often found in the waters of the Gulf. There are a thousand ways to cook it—this is just one I particularly like. The batter makes an extra crispy crust that gets doused by the smoky vinaigrette. I like it served over fresh salad greens for a lovely light supper.

SERVES 6.

6 grouper fillets
Salt and pepper
¾ cup beer
1 large egg, beaten
¼ cup buttermilk
1 tablespoon melted butter

1 teaspoon salt
¼ teaspoon cayenne
3 cups vegetable oil
2 cups yellow cornmeal
Smoked Tomato Vinaigrette (recipe follows)

Rinse the fillets and pat dry. Season lightly with salt and pepper and set aside. In a large mixing bowl, whisk together the beer and the egg, stir in the milk, butter, salt, and cayenne.

Heat the vegetable oil in a deep skillet or Dutch oven to 350°F.

Drop the fillets into the batter and then dredge in the cornmeal.

Fry the fillets for approximately 3 to 4 minutes per side. Drain on paper towels and serve over greens with Smoked Tomato Vinaigrette (recipe follows).

Smoked Tomato Vinaigrette

An update on hot bacon dressing—more savory than sweet.

SERVES 6.

4 slices raw bacon, chopped fine
2 tablespoons olive oil
½ red onion, sliced thinly
1 teaspoon chopped garlic
2 fresh tomatoes, diced
3 tablespoons red wine vinegar

1 tablespoon light brown sugar
½ teaspoon salt
½ teaspoon black pepper
1 tablespoon chopped flat leaf
  parsley

Place the raw chopped bacon in a skillet and cook until the bacon is crispy and has rendered its fat. Remove the bacon from the skillet and add the olive oil. Add the onion and cook 1 minute. Add the garlic and then the tomatoes. Cook on high for 2 minutes, until the tomato begins to break down. Add the vinegar, sugar, salt, and pepper. Stir to slightly emulsify, sprinkle in the parsley, and spoon the vinaigrette over the hot, crispy grouper. Yum!

Grilled Duck Breast with Blackberry Red Onion Jus

appetizers

salads

soups

vegetables & sides

entrees

desserts & pastries

The availability of frozen duck breasts has made them easy to prepare. I always like to score through the duck fat. This allows most of the fat to melt away, leaving a crispy brown skin that's delightful to eat.

SERVES 6.

6 duck breasts
Salt and pepper
Blackberry Red Onion Jus (recipe follows)

Preheat a clean grill to medium.

Rinse the duck breasts and pat dry. Place on a cutting board, skin side up. Using a very sharp knife, score through the fat, just down to the skin, making several diagonal slashes in one direction, and then in the other, forming a diamond pattern in the skin. Sprinkle both sides with salt and pepper.

Spray the grill with nonstick spray, then place the duck breasts on the grill, skin side down. Cook for 8 minutes, then turn and cook 4 minutes more for medium rare. Slice thinly and serve with Blackberry Red Onion Jus.

Blackberry Red Onion Jus

The richness of duck is always nicely balanced by the acidity of fruit. Local blackberries make a beautiful sauce with a little bit of onion for a savory note.

MAKES ABOUT 1 1/2 QUARTS

1 quart fresh blackberries
2 tablespoons butter
½ red onion, chopped
1 cup chicken stock, heated
½ cup plum wine

1 tablespoon roughly chopped
 fresh mint
½ teaspoon salt
¼ teaspoon black pepper

Puree the blackberries in a food processor, strain into a mixing bowl, and set aside.

Melt the butter in a 2-quart sauce pan, add the onion and cook on medium heat for 10 minutes, until very soft.

Add the chicken stock and reserved blackberries, stir, and heat through.

Add the plum wine, mint, salt, and pepper. Taste and adjust seasoning. Serve warm over the sliced, grilled duck breasts.

House Smoked Trout with Watermelon Salsa

Trout is one of our few local fish, here in the mid-South, which most people will eat, at least. Trout is so delicious, almost everyone loves it. In the summer I love to smoke trout for an easy, light entree. The smoky flavor with the crisp Watermelon Salsa is wonderfully refreshing on a sultry summer night.

SERVES 6 FOR A GENEROUS FIRST COURSE OR 6 FOR A LIGHT ENTREE.

4 cups wood chips
½ (12-ounce) beer
1 cup water

Salt and pepper
6 single white belly trout fillets
Watermelon Salsa (recipe follows)

Smoking food is not rocket science. It may easily be accomplished using wood chips on a covered grill. Martha's, like many restaurants, chooses to smoke inside, in a pan designated solely for that purpose. We use a regular stainless steel pan which has a perforated insert and a tight fitting lid. Place the wood chips, beer, and water in the bottom of the pan. Drink the rest of your beer, then season the wood chips liberally with salt and pepper. Spray the insert with nonstick spray and place it inside the pan. Cover it with the lid, and place the whole thing directly over gas burners on low heat. Season the fish lightly with salt and pepper, and wait to see a little smoke escape.

Now you're ready to start your fish. Lift the lid carefully, to avoid getting smoke in your eyes. Ouch! It hurts. Place the seasoned fish on the perforated insert and cover with the lid. Smoke for 5 to 6 minutes. The fish should be just cooked through and still moist. Serve the chilled Watermelon Salsa over the warm smoked trout, spooning some juices around and over the fish, or cool the trout to use in salads, spreads, or tasty smoked trout cakes.

Watermelon Salsa

This is such a nice sauce for any fish, but I like it best with this trout. The freshness of the watermelon and the smoky fish make for a perfect marriage of taste and texture.

MAKES ABOUT 2 QUARTS.

¼ seedless watermelon, diced

2 poblano peppers, diced

½ red onion, minced

2 teaspoon fresh garlic

Juice of 3 limes

1½ teaspoons salt

2 tablespoons fresh chopped mint

Place all of the ingredients in a mixing bowl and toss together lightly.

Vidalia, Tomato, and Basil Pie

Really a quiche, our Vidalia, Tomato, and Basil Pie is probably our most popular summer lunch entree. One restaurant reviewer warned that Martha's "might even make quiche cool again." When was it not?

MAKES 2 PIES, SERVES 8 TO 12.

appetizers

salads

soups

vegetables & sides

entrees

desserts & pastries

1 recipe piecrust (see page 93)
1 Vidalia onion, sliced into thin half-circles
2 cups shredded sharp white cheddar
    cheese
3 ripe but firm tomatoes, sliced ½-inch thick
4 tablespoons roughly chopped fresh basil

15 eggs, lightly
    beaten
2 cups heavy cream
1 teaspoon salt
½ teaspoon black pepper

Preheat oven to 375°F. Spray 2 deep 8-inch pie tins with nonstick spray. Roll out pie dough to 1/8-inch. Roll 1 circle of pie dough onto rolling pin and place over pie tin. Repeat with remaining dough. Fit piecrusts into tins and crimp edges. Place parchment paper over the pastries and weight with dry beans or rice. Place tins in the center of the preheated oven and bake for 12 to 15 minutes, until the edges are beginning to brown. Remove parchment and weights, return to oven, and bake 8 minutes more. Remove from oven and set aside.

Sauté the onion with a pinch of salt and pepper until quite soft. Set aside to cool. Place layers of filling in the prepared piecrusts as follows: onion, cheddar, tomato, basil, cheddar, tomato, basil.

In a mixing bowl, whisk together the eggs and cream with the salt and pepper. Pour evenly over the filled pies. Place the pies in the center of the pre-heated oven. Bake for 40 to 45 minutes, until poofed, lightly browned, and set. Let cool slightly before serving.

Corn Light Bread

The hands-down cornbread winner for picnics and other summer affairs. Corn Light Bread is cakey and dense, which means it won't dry out. A wonderful vehicle for sopping up barbecue and all manner of savory juices.

MAKES 1 LOAF.

2 cups cornmeal

1 cup all-purpose flour

¼ cup sugar

¾ teaspoon salt

1 tablespoon baking powder

1 egg, lightly beaten

⅓ cup vegetable oil

2 cups buttermilk

Preheat oven to 375°F. Grease and flour a loaf pan.

Stir together the dry ingredients in a large mixing bowl. In a separate bowl, stir together the egg with the vegetable oil and the milk. Make a well in the dry ingredients. Pour the wet ingredients into this and lightly mix together. Pour into the prepared pan and place in the center of the preheated oven. Bake for 30 minutes, until risen and lightly browned.

Peach and Blackberry Cobbler

*This is our pastry chef Katherine's favorite cobbler, and rightly
so. The lusciousness of the peaches with the tart and slightly sour
blackberries need very little frou frou to bring out their summery
best.*

appetizers

salads

soups

vegetables & sides

entrees

desserts & pastries

SERVES 6 TO 8.

1 recipe piecrust (see page 93)
6 firm but ripe peaches, peeled and cut into
   ½-inch thick wedges
2 cups fresh blackberries, rinsed and
   picked over

¼ cup plus ¼ cup
   sugar
1 egg yolk
2 tablespoons milk

Preheat oven to 350°F. Have ready an unbuttered 2-quart casserole or baking
dish.

Toss the peaches and blackberries together in the casserole dish. Sprinkle
1/4 cup sugar over the fruit and set aside.

Roll out your pastry to fit the top of the casserole dish. Place the pastry over
the filling and crimp or otherwise finish the edges.

Whisk the egg yolk and milk together in a cup or small bowl, and use a
pastry brush to evenly brush the pastry with the egg wash. Cut a few slits in the
pastry to vent the steam. Sprinkle the top with the remaining 1/4 cup sugar.

Place in the center of the preheated oven and bake for approximately 45
minutes, until the top is nicely browned and the juices slightly thickened. Let
cool for 15 minutes before serving with vanilla bean ice cream.

Summer Fool

I honestly have to say that I'm not one hundred percent sure that this is an authentic fool. But I so love the name, I borrowed it for this fruity, trifle-ey parfait. It's an old fashioned kind of thing, with so much simple charm.

SERVES 6.

1 recipe Brown Sugar Pound Cake (see page 194) or other pound cake, cooled and cut into 1-inch cubes
1 pint heavy cream, whipped with 2 tablespoons sugar

1 quart strawberries, sliced ¼-inch thick
1 quart plus 1 quart blueberries
½ cup sugar
¼ cup cranberry juice
Mint leaves for garnish

Spoon 1 tablespoon whipped cream into the bottom of 6 parfait cups. Then layer as follows: 3 cubes pound cake, a few slices of strawberry, several blueberries, a bit of whipped cream, then repeat, filling the parfait cups.

Place the second quart of blueberries in a blender with 1/2 cup sugar and 1/4 cup cranberry juice and puree.

Top the parfaits with additional whipped cream, then a bit of blueberry puree, and a sprig of fresh mint. Leftover puree may be used with ice cream or on French toast.

Peach Bread Pudding

The peach bread we use for this pudding is a dessert in itself. We just make it super rich by adding cream and eggs and baking once again. A real feel-good kind of dessert.

appetizers

salads

soups

vegetables & sides

entrees

desserts & pastries

SERVES 12.

(for the bread)
4 firm, ripe peaches, peeled and cut into
    wedges
1 cup plus 1 cup sugar
4 eggs
3 cups flour
1 teaspoon baking soda

1 teaspoon ground
    cinnamon
1¼ cups vegetable oil
1 tablespoon vanilla
Zest of 1 lemon

Preheat oven to 350°F. Grease and flour 2 loaf pans.

Place the peaches in a mixing bowl and mash with 1 cup of sugar. Set aside.

Beat the eggs with the remaining sugar until light. Set aside.

Sift the dry ingredients into a large mixing bowl. Stir in the egg mixture, then the peaches, oil, vanilla and lemon zest.

Pour into prepared loaf pans. Place the pans in the center of the preheated oven and bake for 1 hour. Let cool completely before turning out.

(for the pudding)
1 loaf peach bread, cooled and cut into
    1-inch cubes
4 large eggs

½ cup sugar
3 cups heavy cream
1 tablespoon vanilla
Whipped cream to garnish

Preheat oven to 325°F. Spray a 2-quart baking dish with nonstick spray.

Place the cubed peach bread into a large mixing bowl and set aside.

In a separate bowl, whisk the eggs with the sugar until light. Whisk in the cream and vanilla. Pour the liquid over the bread. Mix lightly and turn into prepared baking dish.

Place in center of preheated oven and bake for 45 minutes to 1 hour, until poofed, nicely browned and set. Serve warm with whipped cream.

Summer

appetizers

salads

soups

vegetables & sides

entrees

desserts & pastries

Lemon Cheesecake with Berries

A cheesecake may not be light, but something about this creamy lemon one is terrifically refreshing. A great dessert to make ahead of time—just garnish with berries right before serving.

SERVES 8 TO 12.

½ (12-ounce) box vanilla wafers
6 tablespoons butter, melted
2 pounds cream cheese, softened
1¾ cups sugar
Grated zest of 2 lemons
Juice of 3 lemons
4 tablespoons flour
⅛ teaspoon salt

4 whole eggs plus 1 yolk, lightly
　beaten
8 ounces heavy cream, whipped
　with 2 teaspoons
　confectioners' sugar
1 quart blueberries, raspberries,
　or strawberries (or a
　combination of 2)

Preheat oven to 300°F. Spray the bottom and sides of a 9-inch springform pan with nonstick spray.

Place the vanilla wafers and the melted butter in the bowl of a food processor fitted with a stainless steel blade. Process until smooth. Press in the bottom of the prepared springform pan. Place in the center of the preheated oven and bake for 10 minutes. Remove and set aside.

Mix together the cream cheese and sugar with an electric mixer. Mix in the lemon zest and juice, the flour, and the salt.

Mix in the beaten eggs, being careful not to over-mix.

Pour the mixture over the baked crust in the springform pan. Place in the center of the preheated oven and bake for 30 to 40 minutes, until set. Remove and cool overnight before serving with whipped cream and fresh berries.

Fall

Of all the seasons, fall is the one for which I yearn the most. Late summer days are relentlessly hot. School children sweat at the morning bus stop. Gardeners give up, seeking shelter in the air-conditioned indoors, looking sheepishly out the windows at expiring plants that plead for care. The mellow drama is real. It is a loathsome time of year, the end of summer. Some years it seems as though, the more cheerfully I force myself to look toward fall's relief, the more I am made to wait. But every year, relief finally comes, first with calming, steady rains, then cool nights, and days of crisply-cut, blue skies, and picture-book, white clouds. At last we can breathe again, and run and play soccer, and start choir, and ballet, and take long walks by the lake. When I was a child, I would return from those walks to open the back door and smell my mother's freshly baked bread and simmering spiced tea. Fall, once it finally arrives, is filled with spicy scents and rosy, flushed cheeks. Fall makes you want to start something good.

Potato Cheddar Biscuits with Fried Turkey and Homemade Mayonnaise

We make such a variety of biscuits at Martha's. They are just the perfect vehicle for stuffing with tasty morsels and always a dollop of something to keep them moist. Look for Johnny's Fried Turkey in the Fall Entrees but don't wait until Thanksgiving to try it!

MAKES ABOUT 18 SMALL BISCUITS.

2 pounds new potatoes, scrubbed
   clean
¹/₂ pound (2 sticks) butter
3 cups all-purpose flour
¹/₂ teaspoon salt
1 tablespoon baking powder
¹/₂ teaspoon baking soda
2 cups cheddar cheese, grated

1 teaspoon red pepper flakes
²/₃ cup buttermilk
1 egg, beaten
1 tablespoon milk
Homemade Mayonnaise
   (see page 52)
Johnny's Fried Turkey
   (see page 189)

Preheat oven to 400°F. Prepare a baking sheet with nonstick spray.

Place the whole, clean potatoes on a separate baking sheet and roast until tender, about 30 minutes. Remove from the oven and place in a large mixing bowl. Add the butter and mash. Meanwhile, sift together the flour, salt, baking powder and soda. Mix into the potatoes, along with the cheese and pepper flakes. Add the buttermilk and stir, just to combine. (Expect the dough to be sticky.) Work in enough flour as needed to make the dough manageable. Flour a work surface, and pat out the dough to 1/2-inch thickness. Cut out in 1 1/2-inch circles and place on prepared baking sheet.

Beat the egg with the milk to make an egg wash, and use a pastry brush to brush the tops of the biscuits. Place in the prepared oven and bake for 15 to 20 minutes, until risen and golden brown. Remove from the oven and let cool slightly before stuffing.

To stuff the biscuits, split open and spread bottom side generously with Homemade Mayonnaise. Top with a small slice of fried turkey and remaining half of biscuit.

Bacon, Apple, and Blue Cheese Tart

appetizers

salads

soups

vegetables & sides

entrees

desserts & pastries

I first made this tart for my supper club, when I was experimenting with different toppings for the restaurant. Friends and family always serve as guinea pigs for my culinary experiments. Out of 3 different tarts, this was my girlfriends' favorite. We ate on tables in the backyard on an early fall night, drank wine, sampled tarts, and talked and laughed and laughed. Thank you, Lord, for food and friends.

MAKES ABOUT 4 (8-INCH) TARTS,
SERVES ABOUT 24.

1 cup lukewarm water
1 teaspoon sugar
2 envelopes dry active yeast
1 teaspoon salt
1 tablespoon plus 1 tablespoon olive oil
   plus additional for the toppings
2 cups all-purpose flour
1 cup cornmeal plus additional for dusting

2 crisp apples, unpeeled, cut in ½-inch
   wedges
6 slices bacon, cut across the grain in
   short, ⅛-inch thick strips, cooked about
   ¾ done and drained
1 red onion, slice thinly
2 cups crumbled sharp blue cheese

Make the crust. Place the lukewarm water and sugar in a small bowl, sprinkle with the yeast, and let sit for 5 minutes, until foamy.

In a food processor, combine the yeast mixture, salt, 1 tablespoon olive oil, flour, and cornmeal, and process until the mixture forms a smooth ball. If the dough is too sticky, add more flour, bit by bit, until it forms a smooth ball. After a ball is formed, continue to process another minute. Turn the dough out onto a floured work surface and knead until the dough becomes elastic, 4 or 5 minutes.

Oil a large bowl with the remaining tablespoon olive oil. Place the dough in the bowl and turn to coat the surface well with olive oil. Cover the bowl tightly with plastic wrap and let stand in a warm place until the dough is doubled in size, 1 to 1 1/2 hours. Punch the dough down in the bowl. Fold the dough in half 2 or 3 times, cover again with plastic wrap, and let the dough rest another 30 minutes.

While the dough is resting, preheat the oven to 500°F, dust 2 baking sheets with cornmeal and assemble the toppings.

Divide the rested dough into 4 pieces. Dust a work surface with cornmeal, and roll each piece out very thinly, into approximately an 8-inch circle. Use a pastry brush to brush the top of the tart with olive oil. Next, evenly distribute the apples over the dough, top with bacon, red onion, and blue cheese. Place the pans in the center of the preheated oven and bake for approximately 8 minutes, until the crust is slightly risen and golden brown and the cheese is melted and bubbling. Remove from the oven and let cool slightly before using a pizza cutter to cut the tarts into wedges. Serve warm.

Bacon-Wrapped Shrimp in Cajun Barbecue Sauce

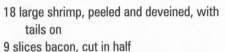

This is our best-selling appetizer for night time at the restaurant. It's embarrassingly simple, as most good things are. After the shrimp are eaten, the sauce remains—a marvelous thing to sop up with some toasty bread. A lingering sort of appetizer, to get the evening started.

appetizers

salads

soups

vegetables & sides

entrees

desserts & pastries

SERVES 6.

18 large shrimp, peeled and deveined, with tails on
9 slices bacon, cut in half
$1/2$ pound butter
$1/4$ cup canned chopped tomatoes
2 teaspoons chopped fresh garlic
Juice of $1/2$ lemon
2 teaspoons paprika
$1/2$ teaspoon Italian seasoning

Pinch cayenne
$1/2$ teaspoon black pepper
2 tablespoons vinegar-based hot sauce
1 teaspoon salt
Sliced French or Tuscan bread for dipping
Chopped parsley (optional)
Lemon slices

Wrap each shrimp in half a piece of bacon and secure with a toothpick. Refrigerate while you prepare the sauce.

Melt the butter in a sauce pan. Add the tomatoes, garlic, lemon juice, and seasonings, and bring to a simmer. Simmer slowly for 20 minutes.

Heat a grill to medium. Place the wrapped shrimp on the heated grill and cook for 3 minutes on each side, until bacon is crisp and shrimp are cooked through. Remove and keep warm.

Lightly grill or toast the bread.

Pour the warm sauce into a serving bowl. Pile the shrimp on top of the sauce and place the sliced bread around the bowl. Sprinkle with chopped parsley (optional) and top with lemon slices.

Fall

Cheddar Spread with Spanish Olives

This is a simple twist on the Southern classic, "pimento cheese." Mind you, I had no idea it was Southern at all, until I found myself living with a bunch of Yankees in the U.S. Virgin Islands. There's not a lot you can rely on in an island grocery store, but you're almost always sure to find a jar of mayonnaise, a jar of Spanish olives, and a package of cheddar cheese. One fateful afternoon I whipped the three together and opened a package of crackers. My friends were stunned and amazed at my culinary prowess. I was just amazed they had never had it. Yet another reason to be grateful for the South.

MAKES ABOUT 1 PINT.

1 pound sharp white cheddar, grated and brought to room temperature
$1/2$ cup mayonnaise
$1/2$ cup pimento stuffed olives
2 tablespoons brine from olives
$1/8$ teaspoon cayenne

Place everything in a bowl and mix well. Keeps covered and refrigerated for up to 1 week.

Martha's Crackers

Fall

At the restaurant, we serve these with Cheddar Spread with
Spanish Olives, and so many other things. I can't tell you how
many of these we go through in a week, although our servers probably could—they're the ones that make them! We use spinach
and sundried tomato-flavored tortillas, mainly because they look
nice together, but I have also used roasted chili, whole wheat, or
even plain white flour tortillas. They're all very good.

    Another variation—I have also made tortilla crackers with
some interesting seasonings, such as cumin and caraway seeds—
quite tasty—but this version works best with all of the different
flavors on our menu.

MAKES ABOUT 75 CRACKERS.

6 (9-inch) flour tortillas
2 egg whites
Kosher salt and cracked black pepper

Preheat oven to 350°F.

    Lay a tortilla out on a clean cutting board. Brush with egg white, then lightly,
lightly sprinkle with salt and pepper. (I explain it to the servers at Martha's as
fairy sprinkles.)

    Use a pizza cutter to cut the tortilla into irregular rectangles, roughly 2-
inches long and 1-inch wide. Place the "crackers" on an ungreased baking sheet.
The pieces may be so close together as to be touching. Place the pan in the center
of the preheated oven and bake until crisp when tapped, approximately 10
minutes. Remove and let cool. Store in an airtight container for up to 1 week.

Sweet Potato Sweetie Pies

In the South, individual fried pies are referred to as sweetie pies. Ours, of course, are different because they're savory—barely sweet at all. They are, however, delicious. Seasoned very subtly and just right. They're perfect for a fall cocktail supper.

MAKES ABOUT 2 DOZEN SWEETIE PIES.

2 sweet potatoes, scrubbed clean
4 tablespoons butter
$\frac{1}{2}$ red onion, diced
1 tablespoon brown sugar
Juice and zest of 1 lime
1 teaspoon salt
1 tablespoon roughly chopped
    cilantro

$\frac{1}{2}$ teaspoon cumin
$\frac{1}{4}$ teaspoon cinnamon
$\frac{1}{4}$ teaspoon cayenne (or to taste)
2 unbaked piecrusts (store-bought
    or homemade), $\frac{1}{8}$-inch thick
Vegetable oil for frying

Preheat oven to 400°F. Place scrubbed sweet potatoes on a baking sheet and roast for 30 to 40 minutes, until quite soft.

Melt the butter in a sauté pan and cook the onion on medium-high heat for 4 minutes, or until soft.

Peel the cooked sweet potatoes and place in a mixing bowl. Add the butter and onion and mash the mixture well. Add the sugar, lime juice and zest, and the seasonings, and mix (it's okay to have some small lumps).

Heat vegetable oil in a deep fryer or a deep skillet to 330°F.

Lay the piecrusts out on a work surface. Cut out 3-inch rounds. Place 1 teaspoon of the sweet potato mixture in the center of each circle. Fold one side over to form a half-moon shape and crimp the edges closed.

Fry the sweetie pies a few at a time until the crust is golden brown. Drain well and serve warm with chutney.

Roasted Fall Vegetables

Fall

I'm always bewildered when people tell me they don't care for the pronounced flavors of many fall and winter vegetables. I think that it's the nip in the air that gives them a bit more character. If you are certain you don't like them because you never did as a kid, maybe it's time to try fall vegetables again.

appetizers

salads

soups

vegetables & sides

entrees

desserts & pastries

SERVES 8 TO 10.

4 cups broccoli florets
4 cups cauliflower florets
2 tablespoons plus 2 tablespoons plus 1
    teaspoon olive oil
1/4 teaspoon plus 1/4 teaspoon plus 1/4
    teaspoon fresh thyme leaves (or just a
    pinch of dried)
Salt and pepper to taste

3 medium carrots,
    peeled and cut
    on the bias in 1 1/2-inch pieces
3 medium parsnips, peeled and cut on the
    bias in 1 1/2-inch pieces
1 red onion, sliced thinly
1 teaspoon chopped garlic
4 tablespoons red wine vinegar

Preheat oven to 400°F.

In a mixing bowl, toss the broccoli and cauliflower together with 2 table-spoons olive oil, 1/4 teaspoon fresh thyme leaves, and a pinch of salt and pepper. Spread out on a sheet pan in 1 layer. Place in the preheated oven and roast for 15 to 20 minutes, until cooked through and lightly browned.

Do the same with the carrots and parsnips together, and then with the onion on a separate baking sheet. (The onion will probably take only 10 to 15 minutes.)

When all of the vegetables are roasted and while they are still warm, toss them all together in a large mixing bowl with garlic and vinegar. Taste for seasoning and serve warm or at room temperature.

Plantation Salad with Roasted Pears and Onions

This salad is extremely popular at Martha's, and rightly so. It makes a perfect entree without being too heavy. The slightly sweet and savory taste of the roasted pears and onions match perfectly with the oozy, melty brie, and the smokiness of the grilled chicken. The leafy greens just make it all seem okay!

SERVES 4.

Marinade (see page 135)
4 boneless breasts of chicken,
   trimmed
2 firm, ripe pears, cored and cut
   into eighths
½ red onion, sliced in 1/4-inch
   strips
1½ tablespoons olive oil

Salt and pepper to taste
Pinch cinnamon
4 to 6 ounces thinly sliced brie
   cheese
4 quarts loosely packed field
   greens
½ to ¾ cup Burnt Sugar
   Vinaigrette (see page 189)

In a large mixing bowl, thoroughly coat the chicken with the marinade. Cover and refrigerate for at least 1 hour and up to 24.

Preheat oven to 400°F.

In a mixing bowl, toss together the pears and onion with the olive oil, salt, pepper, and cinnamon. Spread in a single layer on a baking sheet, place in the preheated oven, and roast for approximately 15 minutes, until the onion is cooked through and the pears slightly softened.

Heat a grill to medium. Remove the chicken from the marinade, blotting it dry, and place on the prepared grill. Cook 4 minutes on 1 side, turn and cook 3 minutes more. Top the chicken with the sliced brie and cover (either with the top of the grill or a metal pan). Cook 2 more minutes, until the brie is melted and the chicken cooked through. Transfer to a cutting board and let cool while you toss the salad.

In a large mixing bowl, toss the field greens with the Burnt Sugar Vinaigrette. Distribute evenly on 4 plates. Place some of the pear and onion mixture around the perimeter of the plates. Slice the chicken in thin strips and place on top of the greens. Serve immediately.

Wild Rice Salad with Oranges and Almonds

Fall

appetizers

salads

soups

vegetables & sides

entrees

desserts & pastries

I think that it's the nutty flavor of wild rice that makes me think of fall. I love this salad, crunchy and fresh, with a subtle bit of curry which gives it the depth a fall salad desires.

SERVES 6 TO 8.

2 cups wild rice
1 teaspoon salt
3 tablespoons olive oil
2 tablespoons rice wine vinegar
1 cup orange segments
$1/2$ red onion, diced

$1/2$ cup toasted almond slices
2 teaspoons curry powder
$1/2$ teaspoon black pepper
1 tablespoon fresh chopped mint

Rinse the wild rice and place in a sauce pan with the salt and cover with water by double the volume. Bring to a boil and cook over medium heat until the rice has just burst open, approximately 30 minutes. Drain and rinse under cold water. Place the rice in a large mixing bowl and toss with the remaining ingredients. Taste for seasoning. Serve warm or room temperature.

Fall

Lentil Salad with Roasted Apples and Spiced Pecans

This salad has surprised me with its popularity. I never knew much about lentils when I was a child. I was probably in college before I'd ever heard of them, but what a great find! They are inexpensive, healthy, quick to prepare, and delicious. They make a wonderful, hearty salad for brisk fall days. When I was in school in Charlottesville, I first made a similar salad for some friends at the Montpelier Races—a perfect match! Lovely for your sophisticated, tailgating crowd.

SERVES ABOUT 6.

2 cups lentils

1 teaspoon salt plus salt and pepper to taste

3 tablespoons plus 1 tablespoon olive oil

1 crisp red apple (Gala and Braebern are my favorites), unpeeled, cut into $1/2$-inch cubes

$1/2$ red onion, halved and cut into $1/4$-inch strips

$1/4$ cup red wine vinegar

1 tablespoon flat leaf parsley, roughly chopped

$1/2$ cup Spiced Pecans (recipe follows)

Rinse and pick through the lentils. Place in a sauce pan and cover with water by double the volume. Add the salt and bring to a boil. Cook over medium heat until the lentils are just tender, approximately 12 minutes. Drain and rinse under cold water. Place in a mixing bowl and toss with 3 tablespoons olive oil.

Preheat oven to 400°F. In a mixing bowl, toss the apple and onion with the olive oil and a pinch of salt and pepper. Spread in 1 layer on a sheet pan. Place in the preheated oven and roast for approximately 10 minutes, until the onion is cooked through and the apple slightly softened.

Lightly mix the apple and onion into the lentils, along with the remaining ingredients. Taste for seasoning. Serve warm or room temperature.

❉

Spiced Pecans

Fall

appetizers

salads

soups

vegetables & sides

entrees

desserts & pastries

2 egg whites
$^1/_4$ cup sugar
1$^1/_2$ teaspoons salt
$^1/_2$ teaspoon cinnamon
$^1/_2$ teaspoon cumin
2$^1/_2$ pounds pecan halves

Preheat oven to 375°F. In a large mixing bowl, whisk the egg whites and the remaining ingredients except the pecans. Add the pecans and toss to coat well. Spread on an unprepared baking sheet and roast for 10 minutes.

Roasted Beets with Blue Cheese and Walnuts

For every person who rails on about their disdain of the poor beet, I find two who are her champion. Granted, I think that beets are one of the "it" vegetables today, on the menus of all the trendy places. But beets have always rocked in cultures around the globe. They are so amazingly good for you, slightly earthy, piquant, beautiful— what more can you ask of a vegetable? Beets are worth making the effort to love.

SERVES 6.

4 medium beets, well rinsed and greens
    trimmed off
1 tablespoon plus 1 tablespoon olive oil
Salt and pepper
1 white onion, cut into ¹/₂-inch circles

3 teaspoons rice wine vinegar
¹/₂ teaspoon minced fresh rosemary
Field greens
4 ounces crumbled blue cheese
¹/₂ cup toasted walnuts

Preheat oven to 325°F. Place beets on a square of aluminum foil. Drizzle with 1 tablespoon olive oil and sprinkle with salt and pepper. Fold the aluminum foil around the beets, securing in a firm parcel. Place the parcel in a baking dish and set in the preheated oven. Roast until very tender, approximately 1 to 1 1/2 hours. Remove from the oven and set aside.

Place the onion circles on a baking sheet, drizzle with the remaining olive oil and sprinkle with salt and pepper. Spread in a single layer and place in the oven. Roast until quite soft, approximately 25 minutes. Remove from the oven and set aside.

When cool enough to handle, remove the beets from the aluminum foil. Slip the beets out of their skins and cut into wedges. Place in a mixing bowl and toss with the onion, vinegar, and rosemary.

To serve, place a small handful of field greens on 6 salad plates. Top each with an equal amount of beets and onions. Top with crumbled blue cheese and walnuts. Serve room temperature.

Fried Green Tomato Salad with Bacon and Roasted Corn

This dish has really gotten people talking. The Fried Green Tomato Salad seems to have stirred some deep-seated craving in Nashvillians and tourists alike. People come up to me at parties and say, "Please! Don't ever take it off the menu!" Of course we do. Being seasonal and all that, we replace the fried green tomatoes with sweet potatoes during the winter and spring. Now people like the Fried Sweet Potato Salad (see page 15), some even love it. But nothing on our menu at any time of year draws the clan of devotees that the Fried Green Tomato Salad does.

For this one, I have to give credit to our first chef, Johnny Swede. He looked at me like I was crazy when I asked him to add fried green tomatoes to the brunch items the summer that I was home with my infant John Mark. Well, once he started frying, Swede apparently couldn't stop. The next time I was in the restaurant, he was serving fried green tomatoes over field greens! Now I never told him to do that, but I'm awfully glad he did.

SERVES 6.

6 green tomatoes
1 quart buttermilk
3 cups flour
3 cups cornmeal
2 teaspoons salt
$^{1}/_{2}$ teaspoon black pepper
$^{1}/_{4}$ teaspoon cayenne
Vegetable oil for frying

4 quarts loosely packed field greens
$^{1}/_{2}$ cup Lemon-Thyme Vinaigrette
   (see page 85)
Creamy Horseradish Sauce (recipe follows)
6 slices bacon, cut crosswise in short $^{1}/_{8}$-inch strips, cooked until crispy and well drained
1 cup fresh or frozen corn kernels

Slice tomatoes 1/2-inch thick. Soak in the buttermilk at least 30 minutes or overnight.

Mix together the flour, cornmeal, salt, pepper, and cayenne in a shallow dish. Remove the tomatoes from the buttermilk and coat on each side with the cornmeal mix. Place on a baking sheet in a single layer and refrigerate at least 30 minutes or up to 3 hours.

Heat vegetable oil in a deep fryer to 330°F. Fry the tomatoes until golden brown, approximately 5 minutes. Drain well.

In a large mixing bowl, toss the greens with the Lemon-Thyme Vinaigrette. Distribute evenly among 6 plates. Top greens with 5 slices fried tomato, drizzle with Creamy Horseradish Sauce, then top with bacon and roasted corn.

Creamy Horseradish Sauce

MAKES ABOUT 2 1/2 CUPS.

2 cups mayonnaise
3 tablespoons prepared horseradish
1 teaspoon paprika

Mix together well.

Curried Mushroom Soup

I've been making this soup in subtle variations for 10 years. Originally, I made it with wild mushrooms. I worked in a market where a large part of my job was using up the produce that was not selling at retail. As much as I love wild mushrooms, I have found that, unless you are a forager yourself, or live in a very large cosmopolitan community, the wild mushrooms you usually find in supermarkets and gourmet groceries are not in very good shape. As an alternative, every day button mushrooms work fine, especially with the heavy seasoning in this soup. You can make this as mild or spicy as you like. The underlying gem is a wonderful roundness of flavor from the earthy mushrooms, rich coconut milk, and sweetly sharp rice wine vinegar. From a gal who is not the creamy soup type, this remains one of my favorites.

MAKES ABOUT 3 QUARTS.

3 tablespoons vegetable oil
$^1/_2$ red onion, diced
1 pound button mushrooms, sliced thinly
1 tablespoon chopped fresh garlic
1 tablespoon red curry paste
1 tablespoon curry powder

$1^1/_2$ quarts chicken stock, heated
2 cups heavy cream
2 cans unsweetened coconut milk
2 tablespoons seasoned rice wine vinegar
2 tablespoons chopped fresh mint
2 tablespoons toasted coconut (optional)

Heat the vegetable oil in a large pot. Add the onion and cook until wilted, approximately 4 minutes. Stir in the mushrooms and the garlic and cook 3 more minutes. Stir in the curry paste and powder and cook 1 minute more. Add the stock, stir, bring to a boil, and cook for 10 minutes.

Allow to cool slightly, then puree the soup in batches in a blender. Return the pureed soup to a pot on the stove. Add the cream, coconut milk, and rice wine vinegar, and heat through. Adjust the seasoning to taste, and garnish with the chopped mint and toasted coconut (optional).

Fall

appetizers

salads

soups

vegetables & sides

entrees

desserts & pastries

Brothy White Bean Soup with Spinach

I absolutely live on soups. I don't make time to eat breakfast, and by the time I've gotten the children where they need to be and arrive at work—about 9:00 A.M.—I am famished. I immediately grab a bowl of soup, and might well have another around 2:00 P.M., when our day business is through. A brothy soup pleases me the most. I'll probably top it with croutons and drizzle on some pesto, but something about the flavor-packed, clear liquid tastes and feels divinely healthful to me. That's why this bean soup is a favorite of mine. It's not super thick and filling, like most bean soups are, and it's got lots of nice vegetables to round things out.

MAKES ABOUT 3 1/2 QUARTS.

3 strips bacon

2 tablespoons olive oil

1 red onion, diced

3 stalks celery, diced

2 carrots, peeled and diced

1 tablespoon chopped fresh garlic

1 (30-ounce) can white beans, drained and rinsed

2 quarts chicken stock, heated

1 teaspoon red pepper flakes

1 teaspoon chopped fresh oregano, or ½ teaspoon dried

4 cups baby spinach leaves, stems removed, roughly chopped

Salt to taste

Croutons and shredded Parmesan cheese, to garnish

Place the bacon in a large pot and cook on medium-high heat until the bacon begins to brown and releases most of its fat, approximately 5 minutes. Remove the bacon and discard or save for another use. Add the olive oil and heat to sizzling. Stir in the onion and cook for 4 minutes. Stir in the celery, carrots and garlic and cook for 5 more minutes. Add the white beans and the chicken stock with the pepper flakes and oregano. Stir and bring to a boil. Reduce to simmer and cook for 10 minutes.

Stir in the spinach leaves and turn off the heat. When the spinach is wilted, adjust the seasoning to taste. Garnish the soup with croutons and shredded Parmesan cheese.

Smoky Corn and Salmon Chowder

This soup is great for the first really chilly night of fall. The smoky flavor comes from chipolte peppers. They are smoked red jalapeños. While the peppers themselves are quite spicy, the yummy sauce that they are canned in—adobo—is relatively mild, but still has that intoxicating smokiness. So, if you want the flavor without the hot, skip the pepper and just use the adobo sauce. You should be able to find chipolte peppers in the Hispanic section of most large grocery stores.

MAKES ABOUT 4 QUARTS.

4 cups fresh or frozen corn kernels
1½ teaspoons plus 3 tablespoons plus 1 tablespoon olive oil
Salt and black pepper
1 red onion, diced
1 poblano pepper, diced
2 carrots, diced
1 tablespoon chopped fresh garlic
1 tablespoon ground cumin
1 tablespoon chili powder
2 quarts chicken stock, heated

1 chipolte pepper minced (with a bit of adobo sauce)
1 (28-ounce) can chopped tomatoes with juice
2 medium yellow flesh potatoes, peeled and diced
1 pound skinned salmon fillet, cut into 1-inch cubes
Salt and black pepper
2 cups heavy cream
3 tablespoons chopped fresh cilantro

Preheat the oven to 400°F. Spread the corn on a baking sheet, toss with 1 1/2 teaspoons olive oil, salt, and pepper and place in the preheated oven. Roast the corn for 8 minutes, until cooked through and slightly browned. Set aside.

Heat 3 tablespoons olive oil in a large pot on top of the stove. Stir in the onion and cook for 4 minutes. Stir in the poblano pepper, carrots, and garlic and cook 5 minutes more. Stir in the cumin and chili powder and cook 1 minute. Add the roasted corn, stock, chipolte pepper, and tomatoes. Bring to a boil, add the potatoes, and cook for 10 minutes. Let cool slightly.

While the soup is cooling, spread the cubed salmon on a baking sheet. Toss with the remaining 1 tablespoon olive oil and a pinch of salt and black pepper.

Place in the preheated oven and roast for 5 minutes. Remove from the oven and set aside.

When the soup has cooled, puree half of it, in batches, in a blender. Stir the pureed soup back into the pot, heat through and add the cream and salmon. Heat through again, adjust the seasoning to taste, garnish with fresh cilantro, and serve hot.

Chicken and Rice Soup with Fall Vegetables

Sometimes it's really worth the trouble to buy a whole chicken, rinse it out, put it in a pot with vegetables and water, cook it 'til it's done, and pull the meat from the bones. I know that this is a radical idea in these days of boneless breast fillets, but fillets will never give you what that whole chicken will—a glorious pot of broth, to say nothing of the most delicious smelling kitchen on your block. And besides, it's really no trouble at all.

MAKES 3 TO 4 QUARTS.

(for the base)
1 whole stewing chicken, neck and giblets
     removed
1 onion, cut in quarters
2 carrots, roughly chopped
3 stalks celery, roughly chopped

2 bay leaves
3 sprigs fresh thyme
3 sprigs fresh flat leaf celery
1 tablespoon salt
1 teaspoon whole black peppercorns

Rinse the chicken inside and out. Place it in a large pot and cover with approximately 2 quarts cold water. Add remaining ingredients and bring to a boil. Skim off any scum that rises to the top, turn the heat to low, and simmer until the chicken is cooked through and tender, approximately 30 minutes.

   Remove the chicken from the pot and place in a bowl or on a plate to cool. Strain the broth into another pot and use a ladle to remove as much fat from the broth as possible. (If you have time to completely cool the broth, the fat turns semisolid, and is quite easily removed.)

   When the chicken is cool enough to handle, remove and discard the skin, then pull the meat, and shred into bite-sized pieces. Refrigerate until you're ready to complete the soup.

(for the soup)
2 quarts reserved chicken broth
2 tablespoons olive oil
1 yellow onion, diced

Inner heart of 1 bunch celery with leaves,
     diced
2 carrots, diced
3 parsnips, diced

1 pint mushrooms, thinly sliced
2 cups shredded, chopped green
   cabbage
2 teaspoons fresh chopped garlic
2 tablespoons rice wine vinegar

Pulled meat from the chicken
2 cups cooked rice
Salt and pepper to taste
½ cup roughly chopped flat leaf
   parsley

Heat the strained broth to a simmer. Heat the oil in another
soup pot, and add the onion. Cook for 4 minutes, then stir in
the celery, carrots, and parsnips. Cook for 5 minutes, then add
the mushrooms, cabbage, and garlic. Pour the simmering broth
over the vegetables, and bring it back up to a simmer. Add the
rice wine vinegar, chicken, and rice, and continue cooking to
just heat through. Season to taste with salt and pepper. Garnish
with the parsley and serve hot.

Split Pea Soup with Ham

Fall

This is a soup for the rumbly in your tumbly. A meal in a bowl, maybe add a green salad. Now, I grew up not knowing what ham hocks were. Maybe you did, too. But ham hocks are out there. They look like a knuckly kind of thing, and they are right there with the rest of the pork in a grocery store. After a ham hock has cooked with the soup, you just peel off the fat, pull away the meat, dice it up, and add it back to the soup. Great, cheap flavor.

appetizers

salads

soups

vegetables & sides

entrees

desserts & pastries

MAKES ABOUT 4 QUARTS.

2 tablespoons olive oil
1 yellow onion, diced
3 carrots, peeled and diced
2 stalks celery, diced
1 pound dried split green peas
2 quarts water

1 beer
1 ham hock
1 tablespoon white wine vinegar
1 green onion, sliced thinly
2 tablespoons flat leaf parsley, roughly
    chopped

Heat the olive oil in a large pot. Add the onion and cook for 4 minutes. Add the carrots and celery and cook 5 minutes more. Stir in the split peas, then add the water and beer, stirring. Add the ham hock and bring the mixture to a boil. Skim off the scum that rises to the top, turn the heat to low and cook, stirring occasionally, until the peas are quite soft and are falling apart.

Remove the ham hock and let cool until cool enough to handle. Remove the ham meat from the hock and dice. Add back to the soup, along with the vinegar and heat through. (If the soup is too thick, you may adjust with more water.) Garnish with the green onions and parsley and serve hot.

appetizers

salads

soups

vegetables & sides

entrees

desserts & pastries

Down Island Fish Stew with Pumpkin

After I finished culinary school in New York, I moved to the magnificent island of St. John for 1 1/2 years. While I was there, I was exposed to so many different tastes and sensations, and people, as well. The Caribbean has been home to a treasure trove of many, many cultures: one dish may speak of the Spanish, African, Indian, French, or Scandinavian peoples—usually a combination of 2 or more. This stew is a testimony to this rich, multi-faceted culture, influenced by all those who have called the islands their home.

MAKES 3 TO 4 QUARTS.

3 tablespoons olive oil
$1/2$ yellow onion, diced
2 poblano peppers, diced
3 cups fresh pumpkin, peeled, and cubed
1 tablespoon chopped fresh garlic
1 tablespoon red curry paste
8 cups chicken stock, heated
Pinch (about 8 threads) saffron

3 sprigs fresh thyme
Pinch ground allspice
2 pounds firm, mildly flavored fish, such as
    snapper, grouper or Mahi, cut into
    slightly larger than bite-sized pieces
1 can unsweetened coconut milk
Juice of 2 limes
Salt and pepper to taste

Heat the olive oil in a large pot. Add the onion and cook for 4 minutes. Add the peppers, pumpkin, and garlic and cook 5 minutes more. Stir in the curry paste, then pour in the stock. Add the saffron, thyme, and allspice and bring to a boil. Cook on medium heat until the pumpkin is tender, approximately 30 minutes. Add the fish and cook until the fish is just cooked through, approximately 5 minutes. Add the coconut milk and lime juice and heat through. Adjust seasoning with salt and pepper, and serve hot.

Spicy Kale

I've had a loyal following for Spicy Kale for almost 10 years. I've been cooking it since my Corner Market days. Now I, personally, have always loved slow-cooked Southern greens. My Daddy's turnip greens can make me cry, they are so good. But even people, not like me, who can't stand the traditional Southern greens, are just crazy about this kale. Maybe it's because I cook it just long enough. Maybe it's all of the garlic, tomatoes, and hot sauce. Maybe it's the beer! Whatever, if I may be so bold, it's really, really good.

SERVES 6-8.

¼ cup olive oil
1 red onion, halved and sliced thinly
2 bunches kale, trimmed and rinsed
2 teaspoons salt
1 tablespoon fresh chopped garlic
2 tablespoons red wine vinegar

1 (28-ounce) can whole tomatoes with juice
1 tomato can water
2 tablespoons hot sauce
½ bottle beer

Heat olive oil in a deep sauté pan. Add onion and cook 5 minutes. Add kale and salt and stir, wilting the kale. Add garlic, then red wine vinegar. Next add tomatoes, water, hot sauce, and beer. (Drink the other half, or give it to a friend.) Cook for 40 minutes. Taste and adjust seasoning.

Roasted Mashed Sweet Potatoes

For those who adore the traditional, really sweet, sweet potatoes, this may not be the dish for you. I rely on most of the sweetening to come from the slow roasting of the potatoes. After that, just a touch of honey and some fresh squeezed orange juice are the only sweetening we add. We do add plenty of butter, some wonderful spices and a bit of heat. To me they are perfection.

SERVES 6 TO 8.

4 pounds sweet potatoes, scrubbed clean	2 tablespoons fresh squeezed orange juice
1 stick of butter	1 teaspoon cumin
Zest of 1 lemon	$^1/_4$ teaspoon cinnamon
1 tablespoon fresh squeezed lemon juice	2 teaspoons honey
Zest of 1 orange	Pinch cayenne
	1 teaspoon salt

Preheat oven to 400°F. Place sweet potatoes on a baking sheet and roast for 30 to 40 minutes, until quite soft.

When cool enough to handle, peel the roasted sweet potatoes, place in a large mixing bowl and mash with the remaining ingredients. Taste for seasoning and serve warm.

Mustard Mashed Potatoes

*In the last 10 years, it seems that Americans have rediscovered
the joy of real mashed potatoes, made from good potatoes, butter,
and cream. Now the flavoring begins. Garlic mashed potatoes are
almost passé (but still really good). I've mashed potatoes with
blue cheese, chipolte peppers, cinnamon, horseradish, and infused
oils. These Mustard Mashed Potatoes are a fairly simple varia-
tion, and awfully good with a traditional roast or ham, or with
grilled meats. The flavor of the mustard is really a bit subtle. You
want to add just enough mustard that your guests say, "Hmm,
there's something really wonderful in here, and I can't quite place
it," instead of, "Wow, there's a whole lot of mustard in these potatoes."*

SERVES 6 TO 8.

4 pounds Yukon Golds, picked over and
   trimmed, as needed
2 tablespoons plus additional salt
1 stick butter

³/₄ cup heavy cream
1 tablespoon Coleman's prepared mustard
¹/₂ teaspoon black pepper

Place the potatoes in a deep pot, cover with water, add the salt and bring to a boil.
Cook on medium-high for 15 minutes, or until quite tender. Drain, then place the
potatoes back in the pot and the pot on the stove. With heat on medium, break up
the potatoes with a spoon to let steam escape. Cook thusly (you don't have to stir
constantly) for about 5 minutes. Remove from heat and mash in remaining ingredients. Taste and adjust seasoning.

❈

Fall

Root Vegetable Gratin

There is something about these earthy vegetables that to me seems very French. Although they are all quite common in true American cuisine, when you choose to feature root vegetables, they seem to take on a sort of "this is me, and to heck with what you think about it," kind of air. I've always admired that in the French. And, when you come to think about it, that's a Southern trait, as well. So, to heck with what you think about it, this gratin is simply divine.

SERVES 10 TO 12.

1 pound yellow flesh potatoes
1 pound parsnips
1 pound sweet potatoes
1 pound turnips
1 large yellow onion
1 teaspoon salt

$^1/_2$ teaspoon white pepper
$1^1/_2$ cups grated Swiss cheese, such as
  Appenzeller or Gruyere
$1^1/_2$ cups cream
Dash nutmeg

Preheat the oven to 350°F. Spray the bottom of a 3-quart casserole or baking dish with nonstick spray.

Wash and peel the vegetables, and slice as thinly as possible. Layer the yellow potato in the casserole, sprinkle with salt and pepper, and top with a little onion and a bit of cheese. Then layer the parsnips, sweet potatoes, and turnips, sprinkling each layer with salt and pepper and topping with onion and cheese.

Pour the cream over the casserole and top with the remaining cheese (if you've run out of cheese, grate another handful). Shake a bit of nutmeg on top. Cover with foil, place in the preheated oven and bake for approximately 45 minutes, until cooked completely through. Remove the foil and bake another 10 minutes, until browned on top. Serve warm.

Baked Macaroni and Cheese

Macaroni and Cheese, as humble as it may sound, is a defining cor-nerstone in my culinary repertoire. It was one of my first food obses-sions: the Macaroni and Cheese made by my grandmother's housekeeper, Catherine Couch. In her Macaroni and Cheese, I first recognized and cherished the prudent use of black pepper. I knew that her Macaroni and Cheese had a custard-like quality, a sense of oneness that did not run, separate, or otherwise fall apart. Couch's Macaroni and Cheese was always a part of our Thanksgiving. I can find no macaroni connection to Thanksgiving with our Puritan ancestors, and am leaning more toward a connection through Couch's African roots. I learned in the Caribbean that no BBQ chicken meal is complete without a side of Macaroni and Cheese. Go figure. Let me know if you know the connec-tion, and let's all give thanks for Couch, her Macaroni and Cheese, and so much more.

SERVES 6 TO 8.

1 tablespoon plus ¹/₂ teaspoon salt
1 pound large shell pasta
1 tablespoon olive oil
2 eggs

2 cups heavy cream
¹/₂ teaspoon black pepper
1¹/₂ pounds sharp white cheddar cheese,
    grated

Preheat the oven to 350°F. Spray the bottom of a 2-quart casserole or baking dish with nonstick spray.

Fill a large pot 3/4 full with water, add the tablespoon of salt and bring to a boil on top of the stove. Add the shell pasta, stir, bring back to a boil, and cook approximately 5 to 6 minutes, until just slightly undercooked. Drain the pasta and cool under cold running water. Place the well drained pasta in the prepared casserole and toss with the olive oil.

In a mixing bowl, beat together the eggs, cream, remaining salt and pepper, and pour over the pasta. Add 3/4 of the grated cheese and mix together well. Sprinkle the remaining cheese on top.

Cover with foil, place in the preheated oven and bake for 30 minutes. Remove the foil and bake another 10 to 15 minutes, until lightly browned on top. Serve warm.

Fall

Plantation Stuffing

The truth be told (and more and more, I find that people like the truth, in doses at least), this dressing was created from my desire to use up leftover cheese grits. Of course, as soon as we started making this dish, business went crazy, and we never had any leftover grits. So, I had to come up with a legitimate recipe. It's not so unorthodox, when you consider that most Southern dressings use cornbread, the kissin' cousin of grits. The ingredients for this stuffing are relatively the same as what my mother uses. I just combine them in a different order. And, of course, I add cheese. Don't wait until Thanksgiving to try out this one.

SERVES 6 TO 8.

3 cups milk
1/4 teaspoon salt plus additional to taste
3/4 cup grits
1 egg, beaten
1 cup shredded Parmesan cheese
3 tablespoons butter
1/2 red onion, diced
1 medium carrot, peeled and diced
1 parsnip, peeled and diced
2 stalks celery with leaves, diced
1 teaspoon fresh thyme leaves (or 1/2
   teaspoon dried)

2 to 3 cups chicken stock
3 pieces day old bread (we use sourdough),
   roughly torn into 1-inch pieces
1 cup roasted pecans
2 tablespoons flat leaf parsely, roughly
   chopped
2 green onions, sliced thinly
1/2 teaspoon black pepper
Pinch cayenne

In a sauce pan on top of the stove, heat the milk with 1/4 teaspoon salt to a simmer. Whisk in the grits and cook, stirring, until thickened, about 5 minutes. Take the sauce pan off the stove, stir in the beaten egg and Parmesan. Pour the grits out onto a baking sheet to let them cool. When cool enough to handle, break up the grits into 1-inch pieces.

Preheat oven to 350°F. Spray a 2-quart casserole or baking dish with non-stick spray.

Melt the butter in a sauté pan and heat to sizzling. Add the onion, carrot, parsnip, celery, and thyme leaves, and cook over medium-high heat until the vegetables are tender, approximately 8 minutes. Place the cooked vegetables in a large mixing bowl, along with the grits, 2 cups of the stock, and the remaining ingredients. Add more stock if you want a wetter dressing. Taste and adjust the seasoning. Serve warm.

Fall

appetizers

salads

soups

vegetables & sides

entrees

desserts & pastries

Fall

appetizers

salads

soups

vegetables & sides

entrees

desserts & pastries

Grilled Pork Loin Chops with Green Tomato Chutney

I love this dish for its simplicity and balance. Pork has a wonderful subtle sweetness, and grilling pork adds a slight smokiness, too. The sweet, tart, and spicy chutney perfectly balances the pork. This is something I serve at home all the time. Even the little kids love chutney. At work we sell this entree for many, many catered affairs. It speaks to the region and is sophisticated without being over-the-top.

SERVES 6.

6 thick cut boneless pork loin chops
2 tablespoons olive oil
1 teaspoon salt
1 teaspoon black pepper

2 teaspoons ground cumin
1½ cups Green Tomato Chutney (recipe follows)

Heat a grill to medium and spray with nonstick spray. Place pork chops on a work surface. Drizzle the olive oil over the chops, sprinkle with the seasoning, and rub the oil and seasoning into both sides of the chops. Place the chops on the heated grill and cook for approximately 8 minutes, turning once. We like to serve the pork slightly pink in the center. You may cook the pork longer to your own desired degree of doneness, but be careful not to overcook. The lean meat will dry out if cooked too long. Serve warm with Green Tomato Chutney.

Green Tomato Chutney

Fall

Chutneys found their way from India to the American South via Great Britain. They may be made from any fruit or vegetable, their common denominator being their aromatic, sweet and spicy flavor. This chutney makes use of the last of the Southern favorite—green tomatoes. While green tomatoes are around from May through November, they are traditionally used in the fall, when tomato growers are gambling over the arrival of the first hard frost and the inevitable end of the season. Chutney is a great way to use up those last tomatoes and preserve the flavor a few weeks more.

MAKES ABOUT 2 QUARTS.

3 green tomatoes, chopped

2 red onions, chopped

2 Granny Smith apples, cored, seeded, and chopped

2 1/2 cups apple cider vinegar

2 cups currants

2 teaspoons mustard seeds

1 teaspoon red pepper flakes

1 1/2 tablespoons salt

Place all of the ingredients in a large, nonreactive pot. Stir together very well and place over medium-high heat. Bring to a boil, then turn heat to simmer. Cook, stirring occasionally, for 1 hour.

Let cool and refrigerate covered for up to 1 month.

Shrimp and Sausage Jambalaya

Jambalaya is a wonderful comfort food. It has so many layers of flavor—the smokiness of the ham, the briny shrimp, and the spiciness of the Andouille, all bound together by tomatoes and rice. Don't be put off by the long list of ingredients. Jambalaya is really easy to make. There are as many recipes for Jambalaya as there are Cajun mamas. I've pulled a few variations from several recipes I've come across. After cooking it a million different ways, this is the Jambalaya that I choose to cook.

SERVES ABOUT 6.

4 tablespoons olive oil
1 medium yellow onion, diced
2 green bell peppers, diced
3 stalks celery with leaves, diced
3 cloves garlic, minced
1 1/2 teaspoons salt
1/2 teaspoon Italian seasoning
1/4 teaspoon black pepper
Pinch cayenne
2 tablespoons tomato paste

2 cups long grain white rice
1 (14 1/2-ounce) can chopped tomatoes with juice
4 cups chicken stock, heated
18 large shrimp, peeled and deveined
1/2 cup shredded, sliced ham
1 pound Andouille sausage (or smoked kielbasa), sliced 1/2-inch thick
1/2 cup flat leaf parsley, roughly chopped
4 scallions, sliced thinly

Heat the olive oil in a deep-sided skillet. Add the onion and cook for 2 minutes. Add the bell pepper, celery, garlic, salt, Italian seasoning, pepper, and cayenne and cook 3 minutes more. Stir in the tomato paste and cook 1 minute more. Add the rice and stir to coat. Stir in the tomatoes and chicken stock, and bring the mixture to a boil. Stir in the shrimp, ham, and sausage, turn the heat to low, and cover and cook for 15 to 20 minutes, until the rice is cooked through. Garnish with parsley and scallions and serve hot.

Pan-Seared Salmon with Curried Leeks and Apples

appetizers

salads

soups

vegetables & sides

entrees

desserts & pastries

We started offering this salmon dish on our fall dinner menu just a few weeks ago, as I am writing this, and it's already become quite popular. I will frequently pair an acidic sauce with salmon to cut through its richness. In this dish, however, we embrace that richness with a slightly sweet and smoky cream sauce. This is a feel-good dish that can take the nip out of a crisp fall night.

SERVES 4.

1 Braeburn or Gala apple, cut into 1-inch cubes

1 leek, cut into thin, 3-inch strips

1 tablespoon plus 1 tablespoon plus 1 tablespoon olive oil

Salt and pepper to taste plus 1 teaspoon salt

1 cup heavy cream

2 tablespoons apple cider

1 tablespoon curry powder

4 (6 to 7-ounce) salmon fillets, skinned and boned

Preheat oven to 400°F.

On separate sheet pans, toss the apples and the leeks each with 1 tablespoon olive oil and a pinch of salt and pepper. Place the pans in the preheated oven and roast for 10 minutes, until softened and lightly browned. Set aside.

Pour the cream and cider into a sauté pan and whisk in the curry powder and 1 teaspoon salt. Bring to a simmer and reduce the cream by half, simmering for 20 minutes.

Season the salmon with salt and pepper. Heat 1 tablespoon olive oil in a large sauté pan. Place the salmon, skin side up, in the sauté pan and sear for 4 minutes without turning. Turn the salmon over and place the pan in the pre-heated oven. Cook for 4 minutes, or until desired doneness.

Plate the salmon, top with the apples, then the cream and roasted leeks. Serve immediately.

Pecan Crusted Trout with Wilted Red Cabbage and Burnt Sugar Vinaigrette

I love to serve trout at Martha's. It's one of our few local table fish, and it's just so delicious and easy to prepare. Here, we match it with another Southern favorite, pecans that have been very finely chopped to form a crust on the trout. The sweet and tangy cabbage gives the dish its bite, to say nothing of some beautiful color.

SERVES 4.

4 (10-ounce) trout fillets
Salt and pepper
3 egg whites
2 cups finely chopped pecans
2 tablespoons plus 2 tablespoons
   olive oil

2 tablespoons butter
¼ red cabbage, finely shredded
Salt and pepper
4 ounces Burnt Sugar Vinaigrette
   (recipe follows)

Preheat the oven to 400°F.

Place the trout on a work surface and sprinkle with salt and pepper.

Place the egg whites in a mixing bowl and beat with a whisk until frothy. Spread the chopped pecans on a large plate.

Dip each trout fillet in the egg whites, flesh side down, and then press the trout, flesh side down, into the chopped pecans. Evenly divide the olive oil between 2 (11-inch) oven-proof sauté pans (or else work in 2 batches) and heat just until the olive oil begins to look wavy. (You don't want the oil too hot or the pecans will burn.) Place the trout flesh down in the sauté pans and cook on medium for 3 minutes. Use a long spatula to carefully flip the trout. Top each fillet with about 1 1/2 teaspoons of butter. Place the pans in the preheated oven and cook for 4 minutes, until just cooked through.

While the trout is cooking in the oven, heat the remaining olive oil in a sauté pan. Add the shredded cabbage, sprinkle with salt and pepper, and cook on high heat until the cabbage is wilted and softened, 3 minutes. Add the vinaigrette to the pan and heat through.

Remove the trout from the oven and place on a serving platter. Spoon the cabbage and the Burnt Sugar Vinaigrette over the trout. Serve immediately.

Burnt Sugar Vinaigrette

This will become one of your favorites. We use it on everything from salads to, well . . . trout!

MAKES ABOUT 2 CUPS.

¾ cup red wine vinegar
1 cup olive oil
2 tablespoons brown sugar
½ teaspoon black pepper

Place all of the ingredients in a blender and blend to emulsify.

Johnny's Fried Turkey

SERVES 10 TO 12 (AVERAGE 1 POUND OF UNCOOKED TURKEY PER PERSON).

My husband John began his turkey frying career at the behest of our dear friend and Southern food devotee, John Egerton, when he and his wife Ann asked us to cater their son March's wedding. The menu (all March's idea) was awesome—from the fried turkeys and catfish to the homemade peach ice cream. The evening was divine—200 happy folk in the Egerton's backyard, complete with August thunderstorms!

But back to the turkeys. We opted to fry the morning of the wedding. I believe there is an unspoken American, if not universal, law which states that anything cooked out-of-doors falls within the male dominion. John, at least, took to turkey frying like a fish to water, and the rest is history. Last Thanksgiving he fried 45 turkeys.

I am perhaps the biggest fan of Johnny's Fried Turkey, and could easily eat a whole one myself—at least all of the dark meat (my fave). The meat stays so moist and delicious—I stuff leftovers into little biscuits for snacks and party food (see Potato Cheddar Biscuits, page 154). Here's how John says he does it.

Fall

appetizers

salads

soups

vegetables & sides

entrees

desserts & pastries

2 tablespoons salt
1 tablespoon dried sage
1 tablespoon garlic powder
2 teaspoons black pepper
2 teaspoons cayenne

1 (10-12) pound turkey, giblets removed, rinsed and patted dry
2½ gallons peanut oil, approximately

Mix the salt, sage, garlic powder, black pepper, and cayenne together in a small mixing bowl. Using gloves, rub the mixture all over the outside of the turkey and up under the skin, as well as in the cavity. Cover, refrigerate, and let sit overnight.

An hour before frying, bring the turkey out of the refrigerator to get to room temperature. Follow the manufacturer's directions to start a propane powered outdoor cooker or turkey fryer. (Note: these may be used only outdoors!) Heat the oil in the pot that comes with the cooker to 350°F. (The amount of oil may vary, depending on the size of your cooker—again, see the manufacturer's instructions.) Position the turkey onto the metal skewer, following the manufacturer's instructions. Carefully place in the hot oil, uncovered, and cook for 3 1/2 minutes per pound.

Remove from the oil and let cool before removing the skewer. Serve warm or at room temperature.

Peppered Beef Fillet with Bourbon Cream Sauce (Tennessee Steak au Poivre)

appetizers

salads

soups

vegetables & sides

entrees

desserts & pastries

It's hard to beat a classic steak au poivre. We just replaced the usual brandy with some Tennessee bourbon to make it more our own. Men love this. (So do I.)

SERVES 4.

4 (7-ounce) beef tenderloin fillets
Salt (to taste)
2 tablespoons freshly ground black pepper

1 tablespoon olive oil
3 tablespoons bourbon
½ cup heavy cream

Season both sides of the fillet with salt. Pour the pepper on a plate and press one side of the fillet into the pepper, coating evenly. (Add more pepper to the plate, if necessary, to coat one side of each fillet.)

Heat the olive oil in a large sauté pan, and add the fillets, pepper side down. Cook for 4 minutes, turn, and cook 4 more minutes for medium rare. Remove the fillets from the sauté pan and keep warm.

Tilting the pan away from you, pour in the bourbon and tilt the pan slightly to ignite. Pour in the cream and swirl it around in the pan. Cook until thickened, about 1 minute. Season with salt.

Plate the fillets and pour the sauce over.

Fall

appetizers

salads

soups

vegetables & sides

entrees

desserts & pastries

Mustard Coated Lamb Chops with Glazed Cranberries

This is a beautiful dish for any festive occasion. The richness of the lamb is nicely accented by the tangy Dijon mustard and tart cranberries. Don't be intimidated by working with the chops. Most major groceries will have them portioned and ready to go. You could put a call in to the meat department ahead of time, just to be sure.

SERVES 4.

2 cups frozen pearl onions
1 tablespoon olive oil
Salt and pepper
1 (1-pound) bag fresh cranberries
4 cups sugar
2 cups apple cider
2 teaspoons salt

1 tablespoon plus 1 tablespoon fresh garlic, chopped
4 racks of lamb (6 ribs together), frenched
2 cups fresh bread crumbs
2 cups Dijon mustard
1 teaspoon fresh rosemary, chopped
1 teaspoon black pepper

Prepare the sauce. Preheat the oven to 375°F. Place the pearl onions on a baking sheet. Coat with the olive oil and a bit of salt and pepper. Roast in the oven for 10 minutes. Remove and set aside. Place the cranberries, sugar, cider, 2 teaspoons salt, and 1 tablespoon garlic in a sauce pan. Bring to a simmer and cook until the berries are burst and the sauce is thickened, about 30 minutes.

Preheat the oven to 375°F. Spray a baking sheet with nonstick spray. Season the lamb racks with salt and pepper. Place the bread crumbs, mustard, 1 tablespoon garlic, fresh rosemary, and black pepper in a mixing bowl and combine well. Evenly coat the meaty part of lamb racks with the mixture and place on the baking sheet, with the ribs forming an arch down to touch the baking sheet. Roast for 20 minutes until medium rare. Remove the racks from the oven and cut each rack into 3 chops. Plate the chops and spoon the cranberry glaze over the meat. Serve at once.

Pumpkin Muffins

I made these for Moriah's kindergarten class, after they had been on a field trip to a pumpkin patch. Only a couple of kids would try the muffins, but they all licked off the cream cheese frosting with chocolate spider webs. The teachers, at least (and Moriah, of course), enjoyed them. Perhaps I'll try them out on seven-year-olds, next time.

MAKES 24 MUFFINS

1½ cups sugar
⅔ cup shortening
4 eggs, beaten
2 cups cooked pumpkin
⅔ cup buttermilk
1 tablespoon vanilla
3½ cups all-purpose flour

½ teaspoon baking powder
2 teaspoons baking soda
2 teaspoons salt
2 teaspoons ground cinnamon
½ teaspoon nutmeg

Preheat oven to 325°F. Spray 24 muffin tins with nonstick spray and line with muffin cups.

In a large mixing bowl, cream together the sugar and shortening. Stir in the egg until the mixture is fluffy. Mix in the pumpkin, buttermilk, and vanilla. Sift together the dry ingredients and mix into the batter. Pour into the prepared muffin tins and bake for 20 minutes, or until a toothpick inserted into a muffin comes out clean.

To make spider muffins, ice the muffins with Cream Cheese Frosting (see page 45). Make Dark Fudge Sauce (see page 39) and place in a squeeze bottle, or purchase chocolate decorative icing. Place 1 dot of fudge sauce in the center of each iced muffin. Make 2 circles surrounding the dot. Place a toothpick in the center of the dot and drag it through the icing to the edge of the muffin. Repeat, going outwards in different directions, 4 more times. Look! It's a spider web!

Brown Sugar Pound Cake

This is my favorite kind of dessert—simple and homey. In the summer I serve it with fresh blackberries, but in the fall, brown sugar pound cake is perfect with Poached Apples with Bourbon (recipe follows) and a little Cinnamon Scented Whipped Cream (see page 41).

2 (9 X 5-INCH) LOAVES, SERVES ABOUT 12.

2 sticks butter

1 1/2 boxes light brown sugar

6 eggs

1 1/3 cups sour cream

3 1/2 cups all-purpose flour

1 teaspoon baking powder

2 teaspoon vanilla

Poached Apples with Bourbon
(recipe follows)

Preheat oven to 325°F. Grease and flour 2 (9 x 5-inch) loaf pans.

Cut the butter into small pieces and cream in a mixer with the brown sugar. Beat in the eggs, then the sour cream. Sift together the flour and baking powder, then stir into the batter. Stir in the vanilla. Pour the batter into the prepared pans, place in the preheated oven, and bake about 45 minutes, until risen, browned, and set. Let the cakes cool in the pans before turning them out.

Serving suggestion: cut 1-inch thick slices of cake, then cut these in half diagonally. Stack the halves on a plate, then spoon Poached Apples with Bourbon with some of their juices over the cake. Top with Cinnamon Scented Whipped cream and a mint sprig.

Poached Apples with Bourbon

SERVES 6.

1¹/₂ cups granulated sugar
³/₄ cup water
2 pounds Braeburn or Gala apples
Juice and zest of 1 lemon
1 cinnamon stick
¹/₂ cup bourbon

appetizers

salads

soups

vegetables & sides

entrees

desserts & pastries

Place the sugar and water in a sauce pan over high heat. Bring
to a boil and stir to dissolve the sugar. Reduce the heat to simmer and cook about
10 minutes, thickening the liquid to a syrup. Meanwhile, peel and thinly slice the
apples. Add to the thickened syrup, along with the lemon juice and zest, cinnamon stick, and bourbon. Simmer for about 5 minutes, then turn off the heat
and let the apples cool in the liquid. Refrigerate up to 2 weeks. Serve warm.

Sweet Potato Fritters

These were on our original lunch menu, and I absolutely love them.
They are not too sweet or heavy—the ricotta really makes them light.

SERVES ABOUT 6, PORTIONS OF 3 SMALL FRITTERS
EACH.

1 medium sweet potato	$^1/_2$ teaspoon cinnamon
1 cup ricotta cheese	$^1/_2$ teaspoon ground ginger
$^1/_3$ cup light brown sugar	Pinch nutmeg
1 cup flour	1 teaspoon grated lemon zest
$2^1/_2$ teaspoons baking powder	2 eggs
$^1/_2$ teaspoon salt	Vegetable oil for frying

Preheat the oven to 400°F. Place the sweet potato on an unprepared baking sheet and roast in the oven until quite soft, 30 to 45 minutes. Remove from the oven and let cool before peeling.

Place the sweet potato in the bowl of a food processor fitted with a steel blade. Add the ricotta and process until smooth. Add the sugar and process. Sift together the flour with the baking powder, salt, cinnamon, ginger, and nutmeg. Add to the food processor in 2 additions, processing after each. Add the lemon zest and eggs and process once again. Let the dough rest for an hour.

Heat the oil in a fryer to 325°F. Spoon tablespoons of batter into the hot oil and fry for a total of 5 minutes, turning occasionally, until the fritters are well-browned. Drain and serve with Lemon Cream Sauce (recipe follows).

Lemon Cream Sauce

Fall

appetizers

salads

soups

vegetables & sides

entrees

desserts & pastries

MAKES ABOUT 4 CUPS.

1 cup plus 4 tablespoons sugar
1¼ cups cream
1¼ cups milk
5 egg yolks
Juice and grated zest of 1 lemon

Combine the sugar, cream, and milk in a pot over low heat
and stir until the sugar dissolves. Set aside. Beat the eggs until
creamy. Spoon 1 cup of the heated milk mixture into the eggs to temper them,
then pour the eggs into the milk. Cook on medium heat, stirring constantly, for 5
to 8 minutes, until the mixture thickens. Remove from the heat and stir in the
lemon juice and zest. Allow to cool and keep refrigerated until ready to use.

Aunt Mary Linda's Burnt Sugar Ice Cream

This old fashioned treat has become a staple at our family birthday parties. The caramel makes an ice cream so rich, you simply have to try it.

MAKES 1 QUART.

1 cup granulated sugar	½ cup powdered sugar
1 cup boiling water	2 cups heavy cream
4 eggs, beaten until lemon-colored	1 teaspoon vanilla

Place the sugar in a sauce pan with 1/4 cup of the boiling water. Cook over medium heat, stirring, until the sugar melts and begins to boil. Continue cooking until the sugar is quite dark. Remove from the heat and carefully pour in the remaining water. This will make the caramel sputter furiously, like a witch's cauldron. When the caramel has cooled somewhat, spoon a little into the beaten eggs, then whisk the eggs back into the caramel. Whisk constantly until the mixture is cooled.

Whisk together the powdered sugar, cream, and vanilla and pour into the cooled caramel. Freeze in an ice cream maker according to manufacturer's instructions.

Over-the-Top Brownies

Fall

For chocoholics and major sweet teeth. This is the "house" brownie at Martha's. We never throw away a scrap. I even use any leftover edges to form the crust on Chocolate Chèvre Cheesecakes (see page 40)!

appetizers

salads

soups

vegetables & sides

entrees

desserts & pastries

MAKES 24 LARGE BROWNIES.

1 pound butter
1 pound plus 1 cup semisweet chocolate
   chips
6 ounces unsweetened chocolate
6 eggs, beaten
2¼ cups sugar
1 tablespoon vanilla

1 cup flour
1 tablespoon baking
   powder
1 teaspoon salt
2 tablespoons instant coffee
1 cup white chocolate chips
1½ cups chopped walnuts

Preheat oven to 350°F. Grease and lightly flour an 18 x 11-inch jelly roll pan.

In the top of a double boiler, melt the butter with 1 pound of semisweet chocolate chips and the unsweetened chocolate. Let cool.

Beat the eggs with the sugar until pale in color. Mix into the cooled chocolate along with the vanilla. Sift together the flour, baking powder, and salt. Stir into the chocolate mixture, along with the instant coffee.

Add the 1 cup semisweet chocolate chips, white chocolate chips, and walnuts and mix.

Pour the mixture onto the prepared pan and spread evenly. Bake in the center of the preheated oven for 30 to 40 minutes. Be careful not to overcook. They should be quite moist. It is best to refrigerate the brownies overnight before cutting. If you'd like to serve the brownies warm, reheat in the microwave for 30 seconds on high.

Acknowledgments

❈

Very special thanks go to Georgette, without whom I would be hard pressed to face the day, to Katherine for acts of faith and friendship beyond the mortal scope, and to Mandy for cheerfully doing all of the things I used to do so that I could do this.

Also to Chris, Silas, Dania, Juan, Ben, Matt, and all of the servers (especially Tim, Pammy, Sandy, Bryant, Ashley, and Lisa-Lou). Thank you for making it happen. Thanks to Alice Randall for making me sound so good, and to Beth Trabue for her photographs that make us look good, too.

Thank you John Egerton for hooking me up with Judy, and thanks to my editor Judy Long, for having the patience of a saint.

Recipe Index

❋

Index